WINNING THE MONEY WAR

WINNING
THE MONEY WAR

LISA DUDSON

RANDOM HOUSE
NEW ZEALAND

For more information on our titles go to www.randomhouse.co.nz

A catalogue record for this book is available from the National Library
of New Zealand

A RANDOM HOUSE BOOK
published by
Random House New Zealand
18 Poland Road, Glenfield, Auckland, New Zealand

Random House International
Random House
20 Vauxhall Bridge Road
London, SW1V 2SA
United Kingdom

Random House Australia (Pty) Ltd
20 Alfred Street, Milsons Point, Sydney,
New South Wales 2061, Australia

Random House South Africa Pty Ltd
Isle of Houghton
Corner Boundary Road and Carse O'Gowrie
Houghton 2198, South Africa

Random House Publishers India Private Ltd
301 World Trade Tower, Hotel Intercontinental Grand Complex,
Barakhamba Lane, New Delhi 110 001, India

First published 2008

© 2008 Lisa Dudson/Cream Media Ltd

Random House New Zealand uses non chlorine-bleached papers from
sustainably managed plantation forests.

The moral rights of the authors have been asserted

ISBN 978 1 86941 998 1

Design: Nick Turzynski, redinc, Auckland
Cover image and images: Cream Media Ltd, images on pp. 17, 23, 78, 109, 117
and 112: www.istockphoto.com
Printed in Australia by Griffin Press

CONTENTS

ATTENTION TROOPS

INTRODUCTION

For many people, money is one of life's worst stresses, making every day feel like a battle for survival. But once you learn how to manage it, money can be one of the most useful tools for helping you live the life you dream of.

The barrage of financial information we face can feel like a minefield we don't know how to cross, and the amount of information is increasing all the time. Winning the money war depends on deciphering that information and learning how to apply it to your situation. The aim of this book is to teach you to control your financial affairs. It contains 122 tips, or battleplans, which are easy to understand, free of jargon, and simple to apply. You can start at the beginning and work your way through, or you can read the tips that are of most interest to you. Everyone deserves financial security. And no matter how dire your financial situation seems, if you really want to you can turn it around so that you feel confident and build success. Like any new habit, it takes some time and effort before new money habits are applied automatically. There will be times when it gets a bit tough, but imagine achieving your financial goals and planting your flag of victory.

Having good financial habits and financial security is incredibly rewarding and can have a major effect on your life. And best of all, it only takes a number of relatively easy and consistent steps. All you have to do is commit to making a change and start today.

FACE THE ENEMY

The first thing you need to do is assess your situation honestly and fearlessly. Ask yourself: what sort of relationship do I have with money?

- I earn plenty of it, but I spend it faster than I earn it.

- I hold on tight to my money and agonise over spending any of it.

- I feel okay with the day-to-day stuff, but am overwhelmed by the bigger things like investing.

- I earn a low income, and am sick and tired of struggling.

- I don't have a clue how much I actually owe, but it's probably a lot.

- I avoid opening any mail that looks like it might be a bill.

- I am always broke, and when I feel down I spend money I don't have.

- I make a reasonable income and seem to muddle through, but I don't really feel on top of things.

- I don't know how to organise my money, and I feel out of control.

- I am always waiting anxiously for my next payday.

- My credit cards are always stretched to the limit.

- I am always borrowing money from my friends or family.

- I'm embarrassed about the mess I feel I have made of my financial situation, and am reluctant to seek help.

Do any of these statements sound like you? Do lots of them sound like you?

Don't worry — you're not alone. Lots of people have trouble managing their money, and they come from all walks of life. People on low incomes and those with extremely high incomes, people of all different educational backgrounds and cultures — they all have to deal with these same issues. And for many people, worrying about money and how to manage it is a major cause of stress and low self-esteem.

The good news is that these problems can all be solved, and everyone can learn to manage money well. All you need to do is take your head out of the sand, make the decision to learn to do things differently, and have the determination to keep going.

Decide today that you are going to make money your friend and have a great relationship with it.

IT'S ALL ABOUT BATTLEFIELD PSYCHOLOGY

Having a positive mindset is the most important tool in the battle to become financially successful and in control of your money. Most people think it's technical know-how that makes people good with money, and they come up with a range of excuses to explain why they're not good with it:

- I wasn't taught about money at school.

- I don't earn enough.

- I'm not smart enough.

- I don't have enough time.

- I don't understand money.

- I'm overwhelmed by too much information.

- I don't have the energy.

- I'm afraid of making a mistake.

- I'd rather wait until some point in the future — which may or may not arrive!

30% knowing what you want

+

35% positive self-image

+

30% attitude that you can do it

+

5% technical know-how

=

Financial success

We create our own reality through our beliefs — chances are that if you are confident that you will succeed, then you will. If you think you can't succeed, then you won't, because you will focus on failure. Our thoughts are based on our beliefs, and our actions are a result of our thoughts. Everything we think and do stems from our beliefs.

You are what YOU believe.

THROW OUT THE NEGATIVE BELIEFS THAT HOLD YOU BACK

- I don't earn enough.

- I don't deserve to have money.

- Money is the root of all evil.

- I will never be in control of my money.

- Managing money is hard.

- Money just seems to slip through my fingers.

- I am hopeless with money.

CREATE NEW POSITIVE BELIEFS

- I can achieve anything I put my mind to.

- I am really good at managing my money.

- I always spend my money wisely.

- I deserve happiness and success.

- I find it easy to manage my money.

- There is enough money for everyone.

- I always earn more than I spend.

Successful people — whether their success is with money, in relationships, in business, sport, or life in general — typically have a great attitude to life. Throw away the beliefs that are holding you back, and reprogramme your mind with positive beliefs that will help you achieve your goals.

Positive beliefs only work if you truly believe in them. The most important things to remember are that you are responsible for your beliefs about money, and that you have the power to change these beliefs.

BELIEFS ⋯▷ THOUGHTS ⋯▷ ACTIONS

MAP OUT YOUR STRATEGY

First, set some goals.

Research shows us that people who set, work towards and achieve goals are vastly more successful than those who don't set goals.

In 1979, the graduates of the MBA programme at Harvard University were asked, 'Have you set clear, written goals for your future and made plans to accomplish them?' Only 3% had written goals and plans, 13% had goals but they weren't in writing, and 84% had no goals other than finishing their course and enjoying the summer. Ten years later the researchers found the 13% who had goals that were not written down were earning, on average, twice as much as the 84% who had no goals. But most surprisingly, they found that the 3% of graduates who had clear, written goals when they left Harvard were earning, on average, 10 times as much as the other 97% of graduates.

For goals to be effective and useful they need to be **SMART** goals: **S**pecific, **M**easurable, **A**chievable, **R**ealistic and have a **T**imeframe. Each time you write down a goal ask yourself the following questions:

- **SPECIFIC** — is your goal specific?

- **MEASURABLE** — can you measure your goal, is it quantifiable?

- **ACHIEVABLE** — do you think this goal is achievable if you are focused, committed and prepared to put in the effort?

- **REALISTIC** — if you are honest with yourself, is it realistic to believe you will achieve this goal?

- **TIMEFRAME** — a task will always expand to fill the number of hours you devote to it, so allocate a timeframe.

DECIDE YOUR SHORT-TERM GOALS

Short-term goals — under two years

Describe your goal	Amount required	Timeframe	Priority	Monthly savings needed
Create my new budget system	$0	Now	1	$0
Pay off all my consumer debt	$12,000	12 months	2	$1,000
Create a 'rainy day' money account	$6,000	3 months	3	$2,000
Save for a new car	$8,000	4 months	4	$2,000

In this example it is assumed there is $1,000 each month of spare cashflow to start with. Once all the debts are paid off, there will be an extra $1,000 each month. Saving for the 'rainy day' account will start after the debts are paid off, and saving for the car will start after the rainy day account has been established.

DECIDE YOUR MEDIUM-TERM GOALS

Medium-term goals — two to five years

Describe your goal	Amount required	Timeframe	Priority	Monthly savings needed
Save for a wedding	$15,000	2.5 years	1	$2,000
Save for a house deposit	$50,000	5 years	2	$2,500

In this example the goals are shared, and it is assumed that both people will have increased incomes over the next few years to enable more money to be put aside for saving.

DECIDE YOUR LONG-TERM GOALS

Long-term goals — more than five years

Describe your goal	Amount required	Timeframe	Priority	Monthly savings needed
Buy a rental property				
Buy a boat				

To make sure the amounts and timeframes for achieving your long-term goals are realistic, it is probably best to state these closer to the time, when you will have a better idea of your situation.

WIN STRATEGIC ADVANTAGE

1. Concentrate on one main goal

Nobody reaches their potential by scattering their energies in lots of different directions — reaching your potential requires focus. You must also decide what you are willing to sacrifice.

2. Concentrate on continual improvement

Each day you can be just that little bit better with money than you were the day before. Each small step will help you get closer to your potential. David Glass, the CEO of WalMart, admired WalMart founder Sam Walton, because, he said, 'There has never been a day in his life, since I've known him, that he didn't improve in some way.'

3. Forget the past

There is no value in looking back at the past. We have all done, said or experienced things we would rather we hadn't. And it's a fact that there is always someone who is a lot worse off. Think of inspirational people like Helen Keller, who lost her sight and hearing when she was 19 months old and went on to become an author, lecturer, and champion of the blind.

4. Focus on the future

As the Spanish proverb says, 'He who does not look ahead remains behind.' Your potential lies ahead of you, no matter what your age, background or situation.

ASSESS YOUR WEAPONRY

In order to take control of your finances and plan your financial future effectively, you first need to establish your starting point. How do you do that? You need to work out what your nett worth is. A nett worth statement is a snapshot of your current financial situation. It will give you important clues about where you should concentrate your efforts.

Let's imagine you have decided to go on a diet, something many of us can relate to. The first thing you need to do is weigh yourself so you know what your current weight is, then you need to decide what weight you would like to be. Once you know this, you can then put a plan together to get you to your target weight. Managing your finances is very similar. And just as the basis of good health and maintaining the right weight is having good eating and exercise habits, to be successful financially you have to have good money habits.

So, first establish your current situation by working out your nett worth. This is the difference between all the things of value that you **own**, and all the debts you **owe**. In financial terms, your nett worth is your **assets** minus your **liabilities**. In other words, if you sold everything today and paid off all your debts, how much money would you have in your hand?

Calculating your nett worth is fairly simple. On the chart on the next page, list all your assets and liabilities in one column, then write the value of the assets in the next column, and the amount of debt (liability) in the third column. Don't include things like clothing and furniture, as they really don't have much value. And be careful about including your life insurance policy, if you have one. You can include its cash value, i.e. what you would get if you cashed it in, but don't include the amount that would be paid out if you died — that's only going to be useful to your beneficiaries, not you.

Complete the table below, adding any other assets or liabilities not already listed, then add up the totals in each column.

Nett worth statement

Asset item	Value (asset)	Debt (liability)
Home		
Holiday house		
Car (1)		
Car (2)		
Boat		
Superannuation		
KiwiSaver		
Life policies (cash value)		
Cash in bank		
Cash in savings account		
Shares		
Term deposits		
Other investments		
Credit card (1)		
Credit card (2)		
Loans to/from family members		
Loans to/from others		
Student loan (1)		
Student loan (2)		
Hire purchase (1)		
Hire purchase (2)		
Overdraft		
TOTAL	$	$

Once you have added up the totals, subtract your liabilities from your assets. If the number is positive (i.e. you have more assets than liabilities) you have a positive nett worth. This is a good thing.

If the number is negative (you have more liabilities than assets) you have a negative nett worth. This is not such a good thing, but it's information you need to know.

Now you know what your starting point is, and you have a way of tracking your financial progress. It's a good idea to check this every year so you know how things are going. It's also a great motivational tool when you see your nett worth increasing over time.

* The average nett worth of a New Zealander is approximately $60,000.
* 16% of New Zealanders have a negative nett worth.
* 30% have a nett worth over $200,000.
* The most valuable asset is residential property, accounting for approximately 43% of total assets.
* The largest debt is mortgage debt, which makes up approximately 80% of all debt.

Source: 2004 Household Savings Survey

AVOID FRIENDLY FIRE

Now it's time to work out where your money goes. In our society we're under constant pressure to spend, being faced with a continual stream of advertisements and enticements. Material things are regarded as important, regardless of whether or not we actually need them, or have the money to pay for them. So let's look at how much of this pressure you give in to, and what you really spend your money on.

Where to start?

Before a realistic budget can be developed you need to understand exactly where your money is going, **and I mean exactly**. So any good budget or spending plan starts with a notebook! The vast majority of people are not entirely sure what they spend their money on, and many have no idea at all. The notebook exercise enables you to work out exactly where your money goes each month. This is one of the most useful exercises you will ever do to help you manage your money better.

Buy a small notebook (a piece of paper divided into 30 sections will also work), carry it with you for a month, and write down every cent you spend and what you spend it on. Quit the moaning and groaning, it's only for one month — you will cope! You will also be surprised by how much money you spend on things without being aware of it, especially discretionary things like meals out, takeaways, magazines, chocolate bars, clothes, etc.

Be totally honest with yourself. The information you gather will enable you to establish a budget — though for the sake of anyone who thinks they have a phobia about budgets, you can call it a spending plan.

We all buy a whole lot of stuff we think we need. Once you've kept your notebook for a month, make a list of the top 10 things you bought during the month that were a want rather than a need. They may be things like:

- buying lunch

- lattes

- cigarettes

- takeaways

- magazines

- videos

- sweets

- clothes

- going out for dinner

- books

Low-sacrifice versus high-sacrifice

Now rank your list according to the level of importance each item has for you. Some will be 'low-sacrifice', i.e. they aren't that important to you, and you really would not miss them. Others will be 'high-sacrifice', i.e. they are important to you, and if you didn't have them you would miss them.

Now you need to decide which items you want to keep in your budget — these will be the ones that are the most important to you. Then you need to make sure they fit into your budget. Those that don't make the final list may be things that you buy only occasionally, when you have some extra money.

SURVEY THE TERRAIN

The key thing is to make a conscious decision about where you spend your money. You can only spend each dollar once — are you really spending your money on things that are important to you? Or could you make better decisions about what you spend your money on?

Budgets should not be too hard. They need to be simple and easy to stick to, otherwise they won't work. Of course it's going to be a little tough in the beginning, just like when you join a gym. For the first few weeks everything aches and you don't like going. During the next few weeks it gets a little easier, and after a month or two you start to miss it if you don't go because it's become a habit.

That's what you are trying to achieve when you create a budget or spending plan. It needs to become a habit, something you don't have to think too hard about because it happens automatically. And your budget has to suit you — there's no such thing as 'one size fits all'. It's important to create a budget that you feel you can stick to. Over the page is a diagram of a system I think is quite effective.

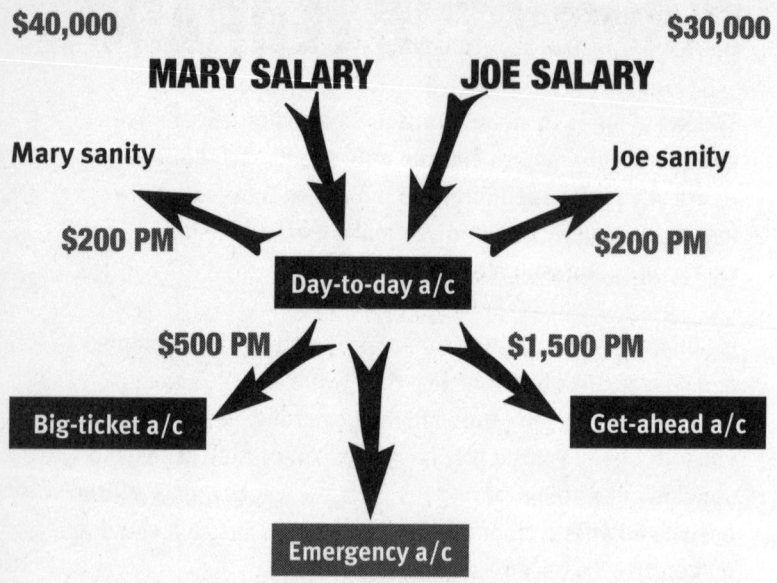

$40,000

MARY SALARY   **JOE SALARY** $30,000

Mary sanity   Joe sanity

$200 PM $200 PM

Day-to-day a/c

$500 PM $1,500 PM

Big-ticket a/c   Get-ahead a/c

Emergency a/c

In this example Mary earns a salary of $40,000 nett (after tax is taken out) and Joe earns $30,000 nett. Together this adds up to $5,833 per month. Both incomes go into their day-to-day account. They have worked out from their notebook exercise that they can live on $3,433 a month, which leaves $400 to be divided between them for 'sanity' money, $500 to go into their big-ticket account, and $1,500 for their get-ahead account. So what do each of these accounts cover?

Day-to-day account

This is the account you use to pay for all the essentials that have to be covered each month (such as rent, mortgage, groceries, insurance, school fees, repayments, petrol, car maintenance, telephone, electricity, etc.).

Big-ticket account

This is the account where you save up for the more expensive things that you would like to have but don't necessarily need (e.g. holidays, upgrading the car or furniture, computer).

Emergency account

Everyone needs some rainy day money. If you don't already have some money set aside for emergencies you will need to put some away each month to build up a rainy day account. See Battleplan 46 for more details on how emergency accounts work.

Get-ahead account

This is the account where you should put as much money as you can afford — this is what will get you ahead financially. If you have any debts, the first priority will be to pay them off. Once you have paid off your debts, this may become the account in which you start saving for a house deposit; once you have your own home you could put money in it to make extra mortgage payments, and/or as part of your long-term savings plan. See Battleplans 80–88 for more on this.

Sanity money

Otherwise known as pocket money. This is the money you can use to buy those discretionary items (wants) that you would like, but don't really need. Looking back to Battleplan 11, use sanity money for the items you have listed as most important. If they don't all fit, some will have to wait until they do. Often the best way to manage your sanity money is to take it out of the ATM in cash once a week, fortnight or month, depending on how you manage your budget, so you know exactly how much you have left to spend. The important thing with sanity money is not to spend any more than your allowance.

The illustration on the previous pages is just one example of how to organise your money, but I have found this type of system to be quite effective. You have to do a little bit of work in the beginning to establish how much money you have and how much you can put in each account, but the theory is that once you have set it up it should be automatic and simple. It's important to set up automatic payments for the amount you choose to put into each account — I don't believe it works when you transfer the money manually, as it is too tempting not to stick to the system.

Setting up your new spending plan is the least enjoyable part of managing your money. However, it is by far the most important thing you will ever do to make you feel in control of your money. If you are on a low income you will have to watch your spending very closely, as you won't have a lot of fat in your budget. But the results of setting up a system that works for you will make it well worth the effort.

DEVELOPING HABITS

⭐ Good money habits are always created consciously; bad habits are always created unconsciously. Your goal is to develop good money management habits that will be with you for a lifetime. Developing new habits can be challenging at first, but once they become habits they are just that — habits! You don't think about them — they are just part of who you are.

⭐ Research shows that it takes approximately 21 days to form a new habit. In the scheme of things, that's not long. So keep persevering and you will have developed a new good habit before you know it.

An extensive survey in the US showed that people spent approximately 20% less when they paid cash instead of using credit. This is apparently because the 'pain' of handing over the cash is greater than that of handing over the plastic. When you pay cash you tend to think more about what you are spending.

DREAM OF VICTORY

Have you seen *The Secret*? It's a DVD and book that has gone around the world at the speed of lightning. Over 1.5 million copies have been sold, and it's selling online at a rate of nearly 5000 copies a day. Essentially *The Secret* is about the Law of Attraction, which says that you attract into your life what you believe and think about.

Battleplan 2 introduced the concept that you are what you believe. A useful tool to help you achieve a positive mindset is a dream or vision board. This is a board that you can create that shows all the things you would like in your life. The simplest way to create a dream board is by getting out a pair of scissors, some glue and a bunch of magazines. Go through the magazines and search for images of your dreams, then cut them out and glue them on a thick piece of paper or cardboard. Alternatively, you can search for the right images on the internet and paste them into a collage on your computer. Your pictures might include:

- your ideal home

- a holiday home by the beach

- riding an elephant on safari in Africa

- your ideal car

- walking on the beach holding hands with two children

- getting into a helicopter

- standing outside a business that you have always wanted

- your dream job.

Have you ever known a successful person who started out without a clue what they wanted in life? A dream provides you with a compass, telling you the direction in which to travel. Without a dream, people struggle to reach their potential as they get stuck in the present.

A dream will provide you with a reason to go, a path to follow, and a target to hit.

A dream board allows you to do two very important things:

1. It gives you a place to focus your thoughts and visualise your desires, while tapping into the universal energy that we all possess and have access to.

2. It gives you the ability to get past your anger, fear and negative thoughts, because you can concentrate on thinking about what you see on your dream board.

Creating your own dream board will not only help you focus on your desires, it will also help you get past limiting beliefs. Your subconscious mind is where this all starts.

Discard the negative

Positive and negative influences on your thoughts, beliefs, attitudes and behaviours come from all directions. Partners, families, friends, colleagues, the media, mentors and role models can all have an effect on the choices you make. It's important to be able to identify where the influences in your life are coming from, and to make sure you absorb the positive and discard the negative.

Do you know people who laugh when you talk about starting a budget, tell you you don't deserve something, or think you're nuts when you talk about your dreams? My advice is to stay out of the path of anyone who is unsupportive or negative, or learn not to pay attention to their negative comments.

KEEP IT SIMPLE

Over time it is easy to accumulate a number of bank accounts that you no longer need. You might not be sure why you have them or what they are used for. One of the keys to good money management is to keep things as simple as possible. Go back to the exercise in Battleplan 12 and decide which of your accounts you really need. The more accounts you have the more you are likely to be paying in bank fees, so unless you need a particular account it's best to close it.

The starting point to managing your bank accounts effectively is to open the statements you receive. It's surprising how many people don't look at their statements each month. It only takes a few moments to check through them, and now that you are starting to feel in control of your money it should be an easy task.

Although it may take a few hours to do a thorough review of all your accounts, the potential bonus is that you could save money in fees, make your life easier by creating a better system or, better still, a combination of the two.

To check what accounts you have, complete the table below. Once you have done this you may find you can consolidate some of the accounts and simplify your life.

Name of bank	Type of account	Fees paid each month	Interest on the account	Balance of the account	Purpose of the account

Some people do find that they manage their money better by putting it into a number of separate accounts. The decision to do this should be based on whether it is worth paying the extra bank fees because it provides you with a better overall result, i.e. you manage your money better. At the same time, check that the accounts you are using are the most appropriate for your purpose. For example, do you have money in a fee-paying cheque account that should really be in an interest-bearing account?

Checklist for managing your bank accounts

How much do you spend on fees each month? This needs to be included in your budget.

- Can you reduce your monthly fees?

- How many accounts do you have? Do you need all of them?

- Does your bank offer any no- or low-fee accounts that you can link to your mortgage account?

- Do you use the internet for your banking? Not only is it convenient, but often the transaction fees are also lower.

- Are your bank accounts with the one bank, to make transfers and internet banking easier?

- Some banks offer no- or low-fee accounts to students, unemployed, children and the elderly — are you entitled to any of these?

- Do you have the best account for your needs?

- Can you reduce the number of EFTPOS or cheque transactions you make by taking out a cash amount at the beginning of each week?

- What interest does your savings account pay? Can you get a better rate?

INCREASE YOUR RESOURCES

Wouldn't we all like to increase our incomes? Take out a piece of paper and start brainstorming ways you could make some extra money. Get creative — every little bit helps!

The Battleplans that follow will give you some ideas.

DO YOU HAVE AN EXTRA
ROOM OR TWO WHERE YOU
COULD ACCOMMODATE A
BOARDER OR STUDENT?
IN THE MAIN CENTRES,
OVERSEAS STUDENTS PAY
$150–200 PER WEEK FOR
FULL BOARD.

PUT THIS MONEY ASIDE
TO **REDUCE DEBT,** FOR
A HOLIDAY OR FOR
UPGRADING YOUR **CAR,** OR
ADD IT TO YOUR **SAVINGS**
FOR, SAY, A DEPOSIT ON
A RENTAL PROPERTY OR
SOME OTHER KIND OF
INVESTMENT.

BABYSIT FOR FRIENDS AND FAMILY.

TRADE TASKS WITH SOMEONE ELSE. A GRANDMOTHER WHO WAS STRUGGLING WITH MONEY PAID SOMEONE TO MOW HER LAWNS EVERY FEW WEEKS, WHILE REGULARLY BABYSITTING HER GRANDCHILDREN FOR FREE. HER CHILDREN WERE FINANCIALLY COMFORTABLE, SO AN ARRANGEMENT WAS MADE WHERE IN RETURN FOR HER BABYSITTING THEY MOWED HER LAWNS.

WHAT **SKILLS** DO YOU HAVE THAT YOU COULD USE TO **EARN EXTRA** INCOME? IF YOU CAN COOK WELL, CAN YOU **SELL HOME-BAKING** TO YOUR FRIENDS AND FAMILY, OR AT LOCAL FAIRS OR MARKETS? IF YOU ARE HANDY ABOUT THE HOUSE OR GARDEN, CAN YOU DO SOME **ODD JOBS** AROUND YOUR NEIGHBOURHOOD?

GET A PART-TIME JOB AT NIGHT OR ON THE WEEKENDS — PERHAPS IN A BAR OR RESTAURANT, A SHOP, ETC.

ARE YOU GETTING PAID

MARKET RATES

FOR WHAT YOU DO?

IF YOU DO A

GOOD JOB

THERE MAY BE AN OPPORTUNITY TO GET YOUR SALARY

INCREASED.

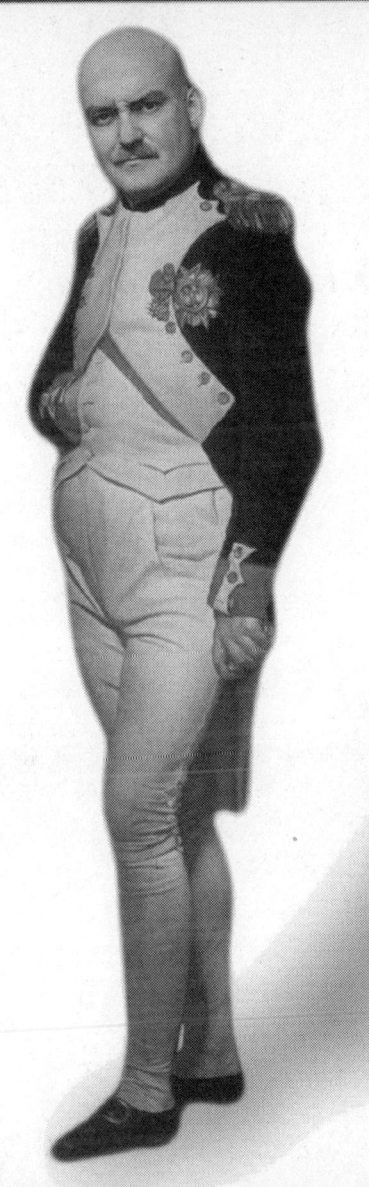

WILL YOUR EMPLOYER
ALLOW YOU TO DO SOME
OVERTIME? EVEN IF IT IS
ONLY OCCASIONALLY IT
ALL ADDS UP.

MOST OF US HAVE STUFF AROUND THE HOUSE THAT WE NEVER USE. HAVE YOU THOUGHT OF HAVING A GARAGE SALE? MAYBE YOU CAN ORGANISE ONE FOR YOUR NEIGHBOURHOOD AND TAKE A PERCENTAGE OF THE PROFITS. WHAT ABOUT SELLING ON TRADE ME?

READ EVERY **STATEMENT** AND **BILL** YOU RECEIVE. QUESTION EVERY **DISCREPANCY**, AND MAKE SURE YOU ARE NOT PAYING FOR SOMEONE ELSE'S MISTAKES. I HAVE PICKED UP **INCORRECT CHARGES** ON MY PHONE BILL, CREDIT CARD AND BANK STATEMENTS, AND I HAVE EVEN BEEN CHARGED CHEQUE FEES ON ACCOUNTS I DON'T HAVE A CHEQUE BOOK FOR! THESE MAY BE SMALL AMOUNTS BUT THEY **ADD UP.**

IF YOU ARE A **LOW-INCOME FAMILY**, HAVE YOU CONTACTED **WINZ** (SEE **BATTLEPLAN 112**) TO MAKE SURE YOU ARE RECEIVING ALL THE **ALLOWANCES** YOU ARE ELIGIBLE FOR?

DRIVE OUT WASTE. BE CREATIVE ABOUT WAYS TO SAVE MONEY AND REDUCE YOUR COSTS. THE BIGGER THE GAP BETWEEN YOUR INCOME AND YOUR SPENDING, THE MORE MONEY YOU CAN PUT TOWARDS DEBT REDUCTION OR SAVING. SEE HOW MANY OF THE FOLLOWING BATTLEPLANS YOU CAN APPLY.

BE RESOURCEFUL.
WHAT'S STORED IN YOUR
CUPBOARD OR FREEZER
THAT YOU DIDN'T KNOW
YOU HAD?

BECOME A CULINARY GENIUS. THINK OUTSIDE THE SQUARE WHEN COOKING. IT'S AMAZING WHAT DELICIOUS FAMILY MEALS CAN BE CREATED USING A STRAY TIN OF TUNA, HALF A CAN OF BAKED BEANS OR THE PEANUT BUTTER AT THE BOTTOM OF THE JAR.

BE LESS WASTEFUL. MANY OF US THROW AWAY AN ENORMOUS AMOUNT OF FOOD EACH WEEK.

BUILD A MENU-PLANNER FOR THE WEEK AHEAD. FREEZE VEGETABLES WHEN THEY ARE IN SEASON AND YOU CAN BUY THEM CHEAPER. DOUBLE THE QUANTITIES WHEN COOKING SOME OF YOUR MEALS SO YOU CAN FREEZE THEM; USE THEM ON DAYS WHEN YOU ARE TOO BUSY OR DON'T FEEL LIKE COOKING, AND AVOID EXPENSIVE TAKEAWAYS.

SHOP SMART. LOOK FOR SPECIALS, DISCOUNTS, COUPON OFFERS AND SALES. BUY AT MARKETS AND CUT-PRICE STORES. LOOK FOR ITEMS WITH DAMAGED PACKAGING, CLEARANCE ITEMS, AND BARGAIN BINS. BUY SPECIALS IN BULK. BUY IN-HOUSE BRANDS OR PLAIN PACKS — THEY ALMOST ALWAYS COST LESS AND ARE USUALLY OF SIMILAR QUALITY.

THINK ABOUT WHAT YOU ACTUALLY NEED. MANY OF US GO ON AUTO-PILOT WHEN WE SHOP AND BUY WHAT WE LIKE, NOT NECESSARILY WHAT WE NEED.

IF IN DOUBT, WALK AWAY; IF YOU QUICKLY STOP THINKING ABOUT THE ITEM YOU CAN PROBABLY LIVE WITHOUT IT QUITE EASILY.

CHECK OUT **MONEYTV'S** VIDEO BLOG ON THE $21-A-WEEK GROCERY CHALLENGE, WHERE THE TARGET IS TO SPEND A MAXIMUM OF $21 PER WEEK ON YOUR GROCERIES — AND YES, **IT** CAN BE DONE!

WWW.MONEYTV.CO.NZ

BECOME A **GARDENER**. YOU DON'T NECESSARILY NEED A **LOT OF ROOM**, AND YOU CAN EAT FOOD THAT'S NOT ONLY CHEAP BUT **SUPER-FRESH**.

IF YOU ALREADY HAVE A **GARDEN** CAN YOU TRADE ANY **EXTRAS** YOU HAVE WITH SOMEONE ELSE?

DON'T SHOP WHEN YOU ARE HUNGRY — YOU TEND TO BUY MORE.

DON'T SHOP WHEN YOU ARE FEELING DOWN — YOU TEND TO BUY THINGS YOU DON'T NEED TO CHEER YOURSELF UP.

USE A **WRITTEN SHOPPING LIST** AND SHOP ONLY **ONCE A WEEK.** THE MORE OFTEN WE SHOP THE MORE WE TEND TO SPEND. GIVE YOURSELF A **SET AMOUNT** EACH WEEK TO USE FOR GROCERIES, SO YOU **DON'T** OVERSPEND.

PAY CASH AND LEAVE YOUR CREDIT CARD AT HOME.

SHOP AROUND FOR BIG-TICKET ITEMS.

ASK FOR A DISCOUNT — IT NEVER HURTS TO ASK.

REDUCE OR CUT OUT TAKEAWAYS.

TAKE YOUR LUNCH TO WORK RATHER THAN BUYING IT.

AVOID VENDING MACHINES.

BUY USED — NEW IS NICE, BUT FOR THE BEST BUYS THINK PRE-OWNED OR PRE-LOVED.

WWW.TRADEME.CO.NZ CAN BE A GREAT PLACE TO GET SOME GOOD DEALS.

BORROW THINGS YOU NEED ONLY OCCASIONALLY, AND TRADE OR SWAP WITH OTHER PEOPLE.

CHECK OUT WWW. SIMPLESAVINGS.CO.NZ, A SITE DEDICATED TO PROVIDING MONEY-SAVING TIPS.

SAVE ELECTRICITY BY TURNING OFF ANY UNUSED APPLIANCES. SEE WWW. CONSUMER.ORG.NZ/ POWERSWITCH FOR TIPS ON SAVING MONEY ON POWER.

GO TO THE MOVIES ON NIGHTS WHEN THE TICKETS ARE CHEAPER.

IF YOU GO OUT FOR DINNER OFTEN, BUY THE ENTERTAINMENT BOOK AND USE THE DISCOUNTS.

KIWI$

"WANT"
YOU

JOIN YOUR COUNTRY'S ARMY!

GOD SAVE THE KING

Reproduced by permission of LONDON OPINION

CONSIDER **SAVING ON HOLIDAY COSTS** BY **EXCHANGING HOUSES** WITH A FRIEND OR SOMEONE WHO'D LIKE TO HOLIDAY IN YOUR AREA.

THERE ARE LITERALLY **HUNDREDS OF WAYS** TO SAVE MONEY. IT'S JUST A MATTER OF **STOPPING** AND **THINKING** BEFORE YOU SPEND. WHICH LEADS US NICELY ON TO THE NEXT BATTLEPLAN.

THINK FIRST, FIRE SECOND

Q. What is the difference between the way a millionaire spends his or her money and the way the average person does?

A. A millionaire spends one minute longer thinking about his or her buying decision.

Before you buy, ask yourself:

- Do I really want this item?

- Do I really need it?

- Can I buy it cheaper somewhere else?

- Can I buy it second-hand?

- Would I get better value if I spent my money on something else?

You get to spend your dollar only once, therefore you need to make sure you get the most benefit from it.

Battleplans 27 to 43 showed you simple ways to save money. While many of them might seem small, it's amazing how the savings mount up. Let's look at the example of taking your lunch to work instead of buying it. Assume that in a week you spend an average of $15 a day on lunch, drinks and snacks. That's $75 per week. If you took your lunch (at a cost of, say, $5 per day) you would save $50 a week. Over a 48-week working year that adds up to $2,400.

That money could be used to reduce debt, take a holiday with your family or pay off your mortgage faster, or be added to a long-term savings/investment plan. What if there were a number of things you could cut back on? Imagine what that would be like.

Next time you go out to buy something, take one minute longer when making your decision. Ask yourself the question: Am I getting the best value for my money in buying this item, or should the money go on something that is more valuable and important to me?

ROOT OUT ENVY

Are the Joneses ruling your life? When those high-living, debt-ridden Joneses get a new car, do you think you have to get a new car too? When they put a swimming pool in the backyard or get a new kitchen, do you think you have to do the same? When they go on an expensive European holiday, do you feel you must follow?

'Keeping up with the Joneses' was originally the title of a comic strip by Arthur R. (Pop) Morand that ran in many US newspapers from 1914 to 1958. The strip chronicled his experiences living in suburbia, where the neighbours were fiercely competitive and continually tried to have the nicest house, lawn, etc. in the street. The phrase has come to describe the practice of competing to maintain an appearance of affluence and wealth for the benefit of others.

The sad implications of keeping up with the Joneses are pressures such as:

- continually having to upgrade to a bigger home

- bigger mortgages

- a new car every three years

- private education for the children

- a better holiday than last year

- multiple credit card debt

- being seen in all the right places

- having the right labels on clothing and household items

- a garage full of exercise equipment and toys you rarely use

- wardrobes full of clothes but nothing to wear

- feeling tired

- never being satisfied.

Don't be fooled by what you perceive other people to have. You will often find that the Joneses either can't do maths or are broke. It is often just a mirage. Behind the expensive cars, houses in the best surburbs and latest designer clothes, they are struggling to get from one month to the next, just like lots of other people.

There will always be people who are better off than you are. And some who are worse off. Get used to it, and don't worry about what everyone else is doing.

ALWAYS HAVE RESERVES

I call it 'rainy day money' — an amount that's set aside in a separate bank account just in case something happens that you hadn't planned on. Effectively, it's an emergency fund. If you get a large, unexpected bill, or if you have to be off work for a while, it's useful to have this money so you don't need to put the bills on your credit card, borrow money from other sources, or face the stress that comes with dealing with unplanned expenses.

How much do I need?

Ideally you want enough to cover your expenses or living costs for at least three months or, in an ideal world, six months. To work out how much that is, look at your budget and see how much your expenses add up to each month. (You should have a budget by now — if not, go back to Battleplans 11 and 12.) For example, if you need $3,000 to live on each month, you will need at least $9,000 in your emergency account. If you need $5,000 to live on each month, you will need to put away $15,000.

What if I don't have this money?

You can start to build up an emergency fund by saving a certain amount from every pay cheque, or perhaps there are things you don't need that you could sell in a garage sale or on Trade Me. Alternatively, liquid assets (assets that you can sell quickly to get cash), like shares or bonus bonds, can be used for emergency money.

You can use your revolving credit or flexi-facility on your mortgage, but remember that you will still have to pay interest on the money you use. I always issue a warning with these mortgages (see Battleplan 70). They can be fantastic tools for managing your money efficiently, but they are best used by people with good financial discipline who track their expenditure and have a clear understanding of how to use these facilities. In my experience, most people don't fit into this category.

If you have a minimum of three months' living costs in an emergency account then you can consider taking a longer stand-down period (the period you have to wait before being paid) on your income protection policy (see Battleplan 77). This can reduce your monthly premiums significantly.

STAY CALM UNDER FIRE

Many people struggle to make financial decisions. There is a whole range of reasons for this — often they just don't take the time, or they feel overwhelmed by the mass of information, or perhaps they and their partner have different attitudes toward money. The following two Battleplans will help.

GIVE CLEAR COMMANDS

When people have different values around money it can affect their relationship. It can also make it hard to make decisions. Try to be clear about what you want to achieve. What is the outcome you want?

If you and your partner have different goals, it may be necessary to agree on a compromise. But how do you find the middle ground where you will both be happy and still achieve the results you want? The first thing to do is to put aside some quality time during which you can discuss the situation. Most people don't do this — instead they have little snippets of conversation in the middle of getting on with their daily lives. How many times have you had this sort of conversation during dinner, while shopping or when driving somewhere? Often this is when one person wants to talk about it but the other is not interested.

Set aside a specific time when you won't have any interruptions, and work through your issues.

DOCUMENT YOUR STRATEGY

Write everything down. This is the best way to avoid going round in circles and getting bogged down in the same old discussions. Make a list of your options and write down all the pros and cons of each one. Which option and list looks like it's going to provide you with the best solution? You're not likely to find a perfect solution, so you will need to decide which one looks best. In most cases you will be far better off just making a decision than not making one.

Putting your head in the sand and hoping the situation will sort itself out is not a good plan of attack. Ignoring it will just make things harder. Remember you can always change your decision if it doesn't work out as well as you had hoped.

ASSESS THE ENEMY

How can you tell if you have too much debt? The obvious answer, of course, is that you either can't make your repayments each month or you are sailing so close to the wind that you get completely stressed thinking about how to make things work.

New Zealand's current high interest rates, the increasing prices of basic items, the high cost of housing and high levels of consumer debt all make it harder for us to manage our money. Excessive debt is a big part of the problem. Could you survive without your next pay cheque? Not being able to survive a missed pay cheque is just one sign that you may be heading for financial trouble.

Do any of the following apply to you?

- I spend more than 20% of my nett income on credit card bills.

- I borrow money to pay off other debts.

- I pay my bills on time, but run out of cash between pay cheques.

- I use my credit card to pay for necessities because I don't have enough cash.

MANAGING DEBT

- I make only the minimum payment on my credit cards. (As a rule of thumb, if you can't pay double the minimum payment, you've got a problem.)

- I've been turned down for a consolidation loan. (This means you have already overextended yourself — your debt ratio is too high.)

- I am refinancing a loan to reduce my monthly payments (for example, you are 24 months into a 48-month loan and need to lower your payments because you are overextended).

- I need a guarantor on a loan. (If a lender requires a guarantor to make a loan creditworthy, it often means you are overextended.)

- I am financing my vehicle over six or more years (i.e. you lower monthly payments, rather than reduce debt).

- I have consolidated my loans but I haven't closed the accounts where the loans originated. (You have retained these as a backup, but if you don't close off things like extra credit cards you're simply compounding your problems.)

- I'm counting on the next 'big deal' to see me through. (You need to look at the big deal as icing on the cake rather than something that's going to bail you out. This includes inheritances!)

- I have more than four credit cards. (There's very little reason to have more than two credit cards. No matter where you go, one or the other will be accepted.)

- I wait until near the end of my credit card's grace period to pay, or I request a higher credit limit.

- I hide purchases, and I fight with my spouse about how to deal with my financial situation. (Financial and domestic problems go hand in hand, or vice versa.)

- I depend on my parents and friends to bail me out.

If more than two of these apply to you, then you need to get on top of the situation as soon as you can.

☆ If you have always paid cash, it can be difficult to borrow money because you don't have a credit history. Conversely, if you always borrow money then you will find it easy to borrow more money. Isn't that crazy? The more you borrow the easier it gets! Don't use that as an excuse to borrow money though!

UNDERSTAND THE ENEMY

In the money war your biggest enemy is consumer debt. That means any debt other than the mortgage on your own home or investment debt (i.e. debt on an asset that makes you money). There are a number of different types of consumer debt.

Type of debt	Lender	Purpose
Personal loan	Bank	Car, home improvements, holidays
Personal loan	Finance companies or moneylenders	Various
Personal loan	Loan sharks	When you get desperate
Overdraft	Bank	Ongoing expenses
Credit cards	Bank	Anything, provided you stay under your credit limit
Hire purchase	Retail outlets	Consumer items
Home loan	Bank, finance company	Property
Student loan	Government	Tertiary education

Fees	Interest rates
Usually 1%	12–20% depending on the bank and what security is offered
Vary	15–30% depending on the lender and the security offered
Huge	Huge — stay away from them!
Set-up fee plus an ongoing monthly fee	15–20% depending on the bank and what security is offered
$20 to several hundred dollars, depending on benefits offered, e.g. airpoints	13–21% (most are around 20%)
Vary; may be no charge; may be set-up fee and/or insurance	Usually around 20%
Vary; usually a loan application fee	7–11% depending on market rates
$50	Approx. 7%

GATHER ENEMY INTELLIGENCE

If you're really in over your head with credit card debt, personal loans and hire purchases and it is beginning to seriously worry you, complete the table below. Then you can begin to work on banishing your debt.

Consumer debt register

Type of debt	Interest rate	Total owed
Credit cards		
Store cards (e.g. Farmers card)		
Hire purchases		
Car loans		
Family loans		
Student loan		
Other		
TOTAL	$	$

	Monthly payment	Annual payment	Total interest cost
	$	$	$

ROUT THE ENEMY

Besides making you feel awful, debt is your main barrier to building a financially secure future. In my ideal world there would be no such thing as consumer debt! However, we live in the real world — so if you absolutely can't avoid consumer debt, then limit it as much as you possibly can.

While it can be discouraging to face a mountain of debt, it's important to remember that there is a way out. The key is to systematically confront your debt with sound tactics designed to accelerate your repayments and reduce the overall interest you pay. Now that you have completed your debt register you can begin. By the time you have paid off your credit card debt you'll have developed a great set of money management skills. You can then put them to work on paying off any other debt, reducing your mortgage, and/or starting a savings programme that will put your money to work to fund your long-term dreams. The following Battleplans show you how.

DO NOT SAY 'CHARGE'!

- If it's not in your spending plan and you can't afford to buy it without using debt, do without.

- If you are having trouble controlling your credit card usage, leave it at home. Or if that doesn't work, imprison it in a block of ice in your freezer. That way you still have it, but there is quite a process to go through to use it. Either way you won't be able to use it impulsively.

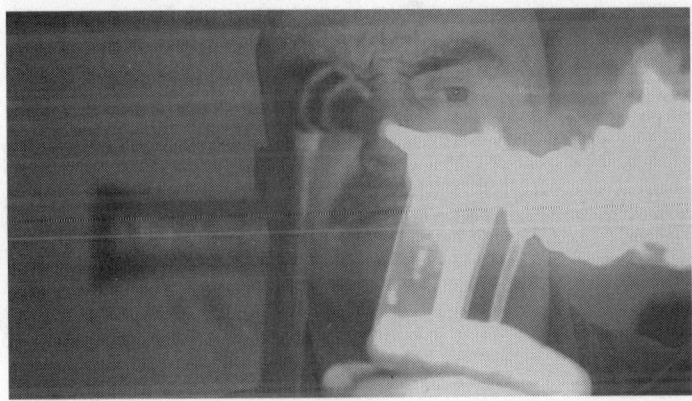

TRENCH WARFARE

Dig into your savings. If you have some money stashed away in a low-interest account (like a savings account), think about using it to pay off some debt. Your savings account will be paying you a low rate of interest, and you'll be paying much more on your debt.

Have a garage sale, or use Trade Me to sell any items you don't use. Use the funds to pay off some of your debt.

Reread Battleplans 15 to 25 on ways to increase your income.

Use any 'extra' money you receive. Whenever you receive anything like a tax refund, gift or raise, use it to repay credit card or other debt. Since you hadn't planned on receiving this income, you won't miss it, and those extra payments can make a big difference.

AN EXTERMINATION PLAN

Start paying off your debts as soon as you can.

Double (or triple or quadruple) payments on your credit card, or the debt with the highest interest. This is the debt that is costing you the most, so concentrate on paying it off first. Once that's taken care of, move on to the debt with the next highest interest.

An alternative is to start with the smallest loan first, then move on to the next one, and the next until they are all paid. This may not necessarily save you the most money in interest, but some people find it the most motivating because they can see the number of debts reducing more quickly. This is because sometimes the debts with the highest interest rates are the biggest.

Whichever method you choose, go back and review the spending plan you developed after reading Battleplan 12; this will help you work out how much extra you can afford to put toward paying off your debts.

WEAPONS MAINTENANCE

Keep going! It's no use paying everything off if you immediately start to load yourself up with debt again. Use your new money management skills to avoid debt and start saving for your long-term goals.

MASS AT THE BORDERS

Debt consolidation means taking out a single loan at an interest rate that's lower than that on other debts, and using it to pay off all the other debts. Generally, the loan will have a stricter repayment plan than, say, a credit card, so while consolidation can be a great idea in that the lower interest rate saves you money, it can also cause you stress. It can also cost you money.

I have mixed views on whether or not debt consolidation works. The lower interest rate can definitely save you money, but in my experience it often just moves the issue sideways. In many cases people consolidate all their debts into one personal loan, then go and put more money on their credit cards.

If you are going to consolidate your debts you need to be totally committed to paying them off, and have a plan in place to do so. Following the steps in the previous Battleplans will ensure you get a good result from debt consolidation.

What about using my mortgage to pay off my debts?

If you have enough equity in your mortgage to do this it can be a good idea. Let's say mortgage interest rates are around 7–10%, which is a good deal lower than the personal loan rate charged by a bank. However, the thing you need to bear in mind is that a mortgage is usually over a 25- or 30-year period. So although the interest rate is lower you will pay more, because you will pay off your debt over a longer period of time.

Let's look at an example:

Type of loan	Loan amount	Interest rate	Period of loan	Payment per month	Interest paid
Mortgage	$10,000	9%	25 years	$83.92	$15,203.47
Secured personal loan	$10,000	15%	4 years	$278.31	$3,355.77
Unsecured personal loan	$10,000	25%	4 years	$331.57	$5,907.25

As you can see, consolidating your debts with your mortgage can lower your interest rate and monthly payments, but because you will typically pay over a much longer period you will end up paying a lot more in interest. This is what I mean by moving the problem sideways. It gives you a payment reprieve, but in the end it costs you a lot more.

If you are disciplined with your money and do decide to consolidate your debts, make sure you stick to your plan and pay them off. If you stay away from the shops and stop getting into more debt you will absolutely save money. But you need to be totally honest with yourself and aware of what you are doing.

AN AMNESTY ON DANGEROUS WEAPONS

There is no doubt that credit cards are extremely convenient. They can also be one of the biggest impediments to gaining control of your spending. It's just too darn easy to use them.

And why would you need more than one? Keeping business and personal spending separate is one of the few reasons you might need more than one credit card. But even then, ask yourself: Do I really need a credit card at all? Or is it way too dangerous?

If the answer to the second question is 'Yes', then take the scissors to it.

If you decide you must have a credit card, then:

- Read the conditions carefully to make sure you have the type of card that suits your needs.

- Set a credit card limit that suits your budget, and resist the bank's offers to raise it.

- Know what the interest rate is.

- Pay off the balance every month (so you won't be paying any interest).

- Make sure you know exactly how much you are putting on your card every month and that it fits into your budget.

If you are still struggling to control your spending, either don't take your card with you when you go shopping (you can always go back if it's really important), or lock it away and only use it in an emergency.

After all, Mathew Barrett, the chief executive of Barclays Bank, has said: 'I don't borrow on credit cards because it's too expensive. There's no question that a credit card is an expensive way to do borrowing. I would not recommend to anyone that they chronically borrow on a credit card.'

If it's not good enough for him, it's not good enough for you!

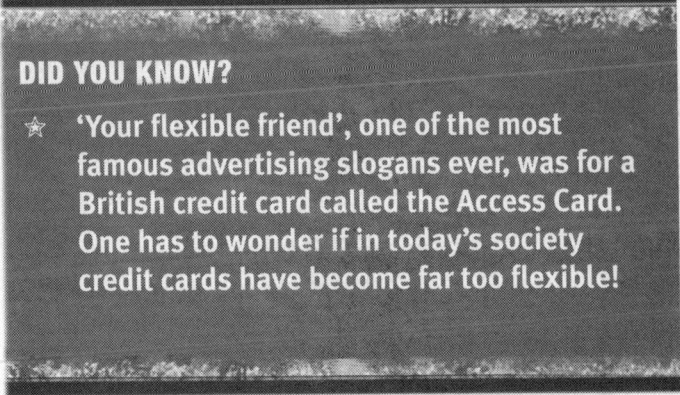

DID YOU KNOW?

☆ 'Your flexible friend', one of the most famous advertising slogans ever, was for a British credit card called the Access Card. One has to wonder if in today's society credit cards have become far too flexible!

CHOOSE THE BEST TRANSPORT

Borrowing to buy a car can get you into deep trouble, very quickly: often the repayments are so high that people are forced to use their credit cards for day-to-day spending, dragging them deeper and deeper into debt. Here are the five most common mistakes people make when buying a car on finance.

1. Not knowing how much car you can really afford

Deciding if you can afford a car involves much more than saying, 'It's only $125 a week.' You need to work out if you can comfortably afford the repayments over the term of the loan. There is, of course, more to the cost of a car than just the purchase price: there are also petrol, insurance, registration, warrants of fitness and maintenance to consider.

2. Buying new vs used

New cars depreciate in value significantly during the first two years of ownership (30 to 40%). If money is an issue (i.e. you don't have the cash), let someone else pay for the depreciation on the first year or two of your car's life: buy used. If you're very concerned about warranties, or determined to have specific options and features, and the rapid loss of value in the first few years of ownership is not a big concern (for example, if you intend to keep the car for five to seven years), buying new may suit you, but go into it with your eyes open.

3. Not knowing the true cost of the deal

You need to think about what the total cost of the deal is. Don't just focus on the $125 per week, work out the total amount you will pay over the term of the loan. You need to include the cost of the interest, as well as any additional costs like loan insurance or finance fees. If you are financing the car from your mortgage remember that you will be paying the loan off over a much longer period of time — so even though the interest rate is lower, the total interest cost will be higher. (See Battleplan 58 for an example.)

4. Choosing a long-term versus a short-term loan

There was a time (not that long ago) when the average term of a car loan was one year. Now, four years is more the norm. Stretching the payments out over a longer term often enables people to buy more car than they can really afford. They also end up paying more in overall interest. Try to buy only as much car as you can afford to pay off in two years — or, even better, in one year.

5. Being upside down on your existing car loan

Long-term loans (and quickly depreciating cars) are also the reason people get 'upside down' on their loan, where they owe more than the car is worth. If they trade the car in or sell it, they have to pay the lender money out of their own pocket, or add the balance of the old loan to their new car payment. I have often come across this in situations where someone in financial difficulties decides to sell their car. Unfortunately they often find that it is hard to justify selling the car, as their debt is now greater than the value of the car.

Having said that, I can't end this chapter without saying ...

CASH IS KING!

In an ideal world you would save up for your car. Set aside an amount in your budget to save toward a car, putting it in your big-ticket account (see Battleplan 12), then go in and pay cash. This will negate any need for finance and cost you a lot less in the long run.

NEW RECRUITS

If you are a student, unless you are fortunate enough to have help from your parents or other family members, you will probably need to take out a student loan. The key is to manage it and not end up with an enormous debt at the end of your study period, and the enormous headache that goes with having to pay it off.

Here are eight really useful rules for student loans from **www. sorted.org.nz**

1. Borrow only what you need
The more you borrow, the more you have to pay back.

2. Explore other sources of money
Is there some other form of income out there that will help you reduce the amount you borrow? Get a holiday job, and/or part-time work during the year.

3. Know the true cost of your loan
It's not just the sum you borrow, it's the time it takes to pay it off and any interest you may be charged.

4. Know the value of your qualification
Putting a dollar value on your earning potential will help you determine if borrowing for your qualification is money well spent.

5. Understand your repayment options

Pay back just the minimum or get rid of your loan sooner? It's up to you.

6. Know your obligations

Be aware that student loans won't go away, and you can't get out of them.

7. Do a budget

Knowing exactly where your money is going is the first step toward controlling your spending.

8. Avoid high-interest debt

Credit cards and personal loans can be very expensive.

Since 1 April 2006, student loans have been interest free for borrowers living in New Zealand for 183 or more consecutive days (about six months). This effectively means that the value of your student loan will stay the same, as interest is not being added. This means that in fact your loan becomes cheaper. If you do go overseas for more than 183 days you will pay interest of 6.9% on your loan.

How does a student loan affect my borrowing position long term?

Note that your student loan will affect your borrowing capacity, as it will be added to any other outstanding liabilities. This decreases your borrowing position, as the amount of your outstanding student loan will be taken into account when the serviceability of any loan you apply for is assessed.

Once you start work

When you start working, you need to tell your employer that you have a student loan and choose the correct tax code so that repayments can be deducted from your salary. If you are self-employed you can make payments directly. You can also make additional payments, which will reduce the number of years it will take you to repay the loan. The IRD website has useful examples, and a calculator where you can input information about your personal situation and see how beneficial it would be to make extra payments.

The repayment threshold for the 2007–08 tax year was $17,784, rising to $18,148 on 1 April 2008 (the threshold is adjusted in April each year). For every dollar of income you earn over the threshold you will need to pay 10 cents toward your student loan.

For more info visit **www.ird.govt.nz/studentloans**

STAY FOCUSED

There may be times when it all seems too hard and you wish you had never made the commitment to getting your finances under control and becoming a good money manager. You wouldn't be human if you didn't have these feelings sometimes. However, the most important thing is to keep taking those small steps every day. You will be surprised how over time even the smallest change makes a big difference.

The following seven Battleplans will help you stay on track.

IF IT ALL FEELS TOO HARD, TAKE A DEEP BREATH AND DON'T MAKE ANY RASH DECISIONS. MAYBE TAKE A WALK, OR TALK TO A FRIEND ABOUT WHAT YOU FIND DIFFICULT. OFTEN WHEN WE TAKE A BREAK THEN LOOK AT THINGS AFRESH THEY DON'T SEEM SO BAD.

DID YOU KNOW?

★ 90% of what we worry about never happens.

TRY TO VISUALISE HOW YOU WILL FEEL WHEN YOU DO BECOME A **GOOD MONEY MANAGER AND ARE IN CONTROL OF YOUR FINANCES.** IMAGINE YOURSELF ACHIEVING YOUR DREAMS. REVISIT BATTLEPLAN 13 AND LOOK AT YOUR DREAM BOARD TO HELP YOU KEEP FOCUSED.

EVERYONE NEEDS SOMEONE TO TALK TO AT TIMES. I OFTEN SUGGEST COUPLES SET ASIDE SOME TIME REGULARLY, EITHER EVERY WEEK OR EVERY MONTH, TO TALK ABOUT THEIR FINANCES. THIS KEEPS THE CONVERSATION TO A DEFINITE TIMEFRAME. IF YOU ARE SINGLE, FIND A FRIEND YOU CAN DO THIS EXERCISE WITH.

WORRYING ABOUT THINGS THAT HAVE HAPPENED WON'T ACHIEVE ANYTHING. I HAVE NEVER BEEN A BELIEVER IN LOOKING BACK INTO THE PAST; AS MY BUSINESS PARTNER SAYS, ALL YOU GET IS A SORE NECK! YOU NEED ALL YOUR ENERGY TO FOCUS ON MORE POSITIVE ACTIVITIES AND TO MOVE FORWARD.

WE ARE ALL HUMAN AND
WE ALL MAKE MISTAKES.
THIS IS OFTEN HOW WE
LEARN. OFTEN IT'S THE
MOST SUCCESSFUL PEOPLE
WHO HAVE MADE THE
MOST MISTAKES.

WHAT WENT WRONG? WHAT DO YOU NEED TO DO TO GET BACK ON TRACK? LOOK AT YOUR OPTIONS AND CALMLY GO ABOUT PUTTING THE MOST APPROPRIATE ONES IN PLACE.

REMEMBER, SUCCESS COMES ONE STEP AT A TIME. REVIEW YOUR GOALS AND SET NEW ONES. YOU CAN ALWAYS START BY DOING ONE THING, THEN ADD SOMETHING ELSE LATER. MANY PEOPLE GET INTO DIFFICULTIES BECAUSE THEY TRY DOING TOO MANY THINGS AT ONCE AND IT GETS TOO HARD. START WITH SMALL STEPS. TRY USING AFFIRMATIONS TO KEEP YOU FOCUSED, ON TRACK AND POSITIVE.

CALL IN THE CAVALRY

For most people, not only is their home their biggest asset, it's also the largest single expenditure they will make in life. So it's important to put some thought into your mortgage. It's not just a matter of rocking up to the bank and asking for a mortgage. There are a number of things to consider.

Which mortgage?

Do you want a principal and interest mortgage (where the mortgage is gradually paid off over a period of time) or an interest-only mortgage (where only the interest is paid). Over time it has been rare for people to take out interest-only mortgages, but in recent years the numbers have increased because housing has become more expensive. This is a real concern. While the repayments are lower with an interest-only mortgage, and therefore more affordable, the danger is that you don't pay off the principal and your mortgage does not get any lower.

Some people use interest-only mortgages to get them through a 'tight spot', with the aim of changing back to a principal and interest mortgage when their finances improve — the trouble is that many of them never seem to get around to making this important change! You need to think extremely seriously before taking out an interest-only mortgage on your own home.

How long do you want your mortgage for?

Traditionally mortgages have been taken out for a 25-year term, although today more and more people are choosing a 30-year term. The longer term means your regular monthly payments are lower, but over the long term you pay much more because you are paying interest for longer. For example, on a $250,000 mortgage at 9%, the total cost of the interest (not including repaying the amount you borrowed, or principal) is $380,096 for a 25-year term and $475,425 for a 30-year term — that's a whopping difference of $95,329! Ideally you want to pay off your mortgage as fast as you can, and reduce the amount of total interest you pay (see Battleplan 72).

What type of mortgage?

There are three main types of mortgage:

1. A fixed mortgage is one where the interest rate is set for a specific length of time, usually between six months and five years, with the most common being two or three years. The advantage of a fixed rate is that you know exactly what your repayments will be for the length of time you have set, which makes it easier to budget. The downside is that you are limited in the number of extra payments you can make if you want to pay off your mortgage faster.

2. A floating or variable mortgage is one where the interest rate goes up or down depending on what the market is doing. This means your repayments will increase or decrease if your lender changes their floating rates; i.e. when interest rates go up your repayments go up, when interest rates go down your repayments go down. This can make it more difficult to budget for your mortgage payments. One advantage of this type of mortgage is that they are more flexible if you want to increase your regular payments or pay a lump sum.

3. Revolving-credit mortgages have a number of variations, and have different names, but basically they give you the structure of a regular principal repayment schedule with the flexibility to repay as much as you like — you can pay off as much of the principal as you like each month or simply pay the interest, and you can reborrow up to your limit any time you like, giving you continuing access to credit. Since interest is calculated daily and charged monthly, the lower your average daily loan balance, the less interest you are charged. This type of mortgage is a great tool to help you pay off your mortgage faster. However, it is only for the very disciplined, as effectively it works like an overdraft.

How much can you afford?

This is the big question, particularly at this time when both interest rates and house prices are very high. Sit down and work through what is realistic and comfortable for you. Some people are currently using up to 50–60% of their after-tax income to pay their mortgage; some are paying a lot less. Don't overcommit yourself or you will be living on baked beans!

Paying your mortgage fortnightly instead of monthly

If you pay your mortgage fortnightly rather than monthly you will save on interest over the long term. By making 26 payments instead of 12 you pay back slightly more principal over the course of a year, and are therefore paying off your mortgage more quickly and saving interest. Before committing to this approach you need to consider how it fits into your budget cycle (i.e., if you work on a weekly, fortnightly or monthly budget) or you might want to take it into account when setting up your budget.

Structuring your mortgage

Many people believe that getting the lowest interest rate is the most important part of getting a mortgage. This is not necessarily the case. Many people fix their entire mortgage, say for three years, and make the required monthly payments, when they could afford much more. An alternative is to have part of your mortgage fixed and part floating; even if you are paying a higher overall interest rate, this can often save you thousands if you end up paying off more of the principal sooner. (See Battleplan 72).

Taking out a mortgage is one of the biggest financial commitments you will ever make. If you put some thought into how your mortgage is structured you can make sure it is the most appropriate for your needs, and you may also save a lot of money over time. Get some advice from a mortgage broker or your bank to make sure the mortgage you get is the best one for you.

Interest & principal

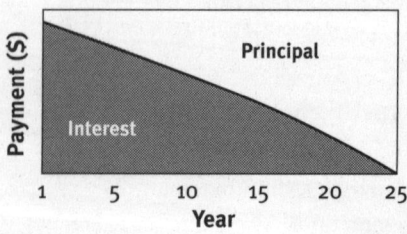

Interest only

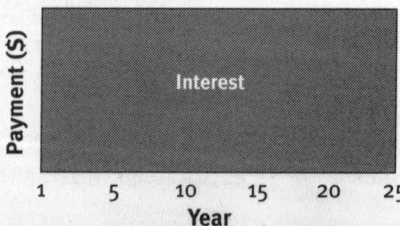

AVOID THE MINEFIELD

A low-equity fee (sometimes called a low-equity premium) is a fee your bank charges if you borrow over 80% of the value of a property. It is sometimes referred to as a mortgage indemnity insurance fee.

Why do they charge it?

The low-equity fee is charged because the bank believes the loan is a higher risk than if it was 80% or less of the value of a property. The low-equity fee is effectively an insurance for the bank. If you get into trouble and have to default on your payments, it has a 20% buffer or margin so that if it has to sell the property it can be pretty certain of getting all its money back. For instance, if you buy a house for $100,000 and borrow $80,000, as long as the bank gets at least $80,000 if it has to sell the house at a mortgagee sale then it won't lose any money. If it sells it for less than $80,000, then the reinsurers will cover the loss.

How does it work?

The fee is worked out using a sliding scale — the higher the percentage you borrow, the higher the fee you pay. For example, using ASB Bank figures:

Amount of loan	Fee when 85% borrowed	Fee when 90% borrowed	Fee when 95% borrowed
$200,000	$1,000	$1,500	$2,000
$400,000	$2,000	$3,000	$4,000

Do I have to pay the fee upfront?

Not usually — most lenders will add it to the total value of your loan. However, if we take a low-equity fee of $3,000, an interest rate of 9% and a term of 25 years, then the total cost of this $3,000 fee over the term of your mortgage would be $7,558 ($3,000 + $4,558 in interest).

In an ideal world you would have a minimum of 20% deposit, but we don't always live in an ideal world, and the high price of houses at the moment makes it particularly difficult. The thing to remember is that the higher your deposit, the lower the low-equity fee (if you are borrowing more than 80%). Recently some banks have only been applying the fee for borrowings over 90%, and in some cases the fee is negotiable — so it pays to ask if it can be lowered or waived.

FORCED MARCHES

Paying off your mortgage faster is a fantastic way to get ahead financially. By accelerating your payments you can save thousands of dollars off the cost of a normal 25-year loan. Most people don't realise the significance of these additional payments and how they add up over a period of time, regardless of how small they may be. They tend to go on paying the standard minimum payments over a 25- or 30-year term, partly out of habit and partly because they have no idea how much interest they will save by fast-tracking their payments.

Most bank and mortgage-broking websites have simple calculators that you can use to work out how much your mortgage is costing you. Here's one example:

$200,000 mortgage	25 years	20 years	15 years	10 years
Interest rate	8.5%	8.5%	8.5%	8.5%
Monthly payment	$1,610	$1,735	$1,969	$2,479
Total interest paid	$283,625	$216,804	$154,613	$97,588

So, in the example above, let's look first at the 25-year column. Assuming an interest rate of 8.5%, the monthly repayment is $1,610 and the total amount of interest paid over the 25-year term is $283,625 — and that's on top of the original $200,000 you borrowed!

In the 20-year column, you will see that if you increase your payments from $1,610 to $1,735 per month (an additional $125) you will save yourself $66,821 in interest over the period of your loan and it will be paid off five years earlier.

Moving along to the 15-year column, increasing your payments from $1,610 to $1,969 per month (an additional $359) will save you $129,012 in interest and your loan will be paid off 10 years earlier.

And if you have quite a bit of extra income available, the 10-year column shows that if you increase your monthly payments from $1,610 to $2,479 (an additional $869), you will save $186,037 in total interest and your loan will be paid off in 10 years rather than 25 years — meaning you will have an extra 15 years of not having to pay $1,610 a month.

It is clear from this example what a big difference those extra payments make over a length of time. Don't underestimate the money you will save by doing this. Most people are not only astounded by the amount they will save, but they also suddenly develop a strong motivation to pay off their mortgage much faster. Even if all you can afford is an extra $10 a week (and that's only about two lattes) the money you save will be well worth it in the long run.

TIP

★ When you take out your mortgage, work out what different interest rates will mean to your payments; i.e., look at the repayments at 7.5%, 8%, 8.5%, 9% and 9.5% and see if you are comfortable with the repayments at these levels.

★ Interest on a floating or variable mortgage can go up at short notice. The interest on a fixed mortgage may go up at the end of its term.

LEAVE INSTRUCTIONS

As the saying goes, there are two things in life that are inevitable: death and taxes. Having a will ensures that when you die your assets are distributed as you want them to be. It can also provide certainty and comfort to those you leave behind, making things a lot simpler for them and minimising the likelihood of disagreement among family members. If you have children, you can appoint a guardian and outline the provisions you have made for them.

LAW AND INSURANCE

A surprising number of New Zealanders do not have a will. In addition, even among people who have wills there are many who haven't updated them in years. Some of the reasons people give for not having a will are:

- I'm too young.

- My family already knows my wishes.

- I don't own enough to give anything away.

- I don't have kids yet.

- I'm single and don't have a partner or children.

- I'm married and my partner and I own half each of all our assets.

- Wills are too expensive to make.

- I'm too busy right now; there's plenty of time later.

- I don't want to think about dying.

- I can't decide what to leave my relatives so I'll wait until I have made a decision.

If you don't have a will, the state deems that you have died intestate. It can then take a long time and cost a lot of money to sort out your estate. After any debts and costs have been paid, your estate will be divided among your relatives. As a result, your wishes may not be carried out.

Once you have a will you should review it about every three years, or when there is a significant change in your circumstances, such as:

- marriage or remarriage

- separation, divorce, starting a de facto relationship

- birth of children or grandchildren

- special needs of dependants

- when setting up a family trust

- acquisition or disposal of a major asset

- death of a loved one.

You can have a will drawn up by your lawyer, or by a public trustee company like the Public Trust, Guardian Trust or Perpetual Trust. I advise caution if you are considering using any of the DIY will kits that are available, as essentially you are not receiving any advice.

A will is a relatively simple document, and unless your affairs are particularly complex it won't take a lot of time or money to draw one up. Compare that to the amount of stress you will cause your family if you don't have one when you die!

SUPPORT WHEN THE GOING GETS TOUGH

Most people think that being married, in a relationship, or being a family member gives you the legal right to make decisions for your spouse, partner, parent, etc. This is not the case.

If you don't have an Enduring Power of Attorney (EPA) in place, and you become mentally incapacitated and unable to manage your affairs, an application will need to be made to the Family Court. The court then decides who is to be appointed as your attorney. This will not necessarily be the person you would have wanted appointed. Here's an example I've come across:

Scott (35) worked in a timber mill. He was married and had two young children. One day Scott was caught in a piece of machinery at work, and received severe head injuries. Scott was mentally incapable of making decisions for himself. With no EPA in place the Family Court was approached and asked to appoint his wife Sarah as his attorney. Scott's family fought the appointment, and the issue was dragged through the court. Although Sarah was ultimately successful, had Scott completed an EPA earlier he would have saved his wife and children the stress and significant cost of having to go through the court.

Illness or an accident like Scott's can happen at any time. Setting up an Enduring Power of Attorney, appointing somebody you trust to take care of your affairs, enables you to make important decisions and choices while you are still in control.

There are two types of EPA: an Enduring Power of Attorney in relation to Property and an Enduring Power of Attorney in relation to Personal Care and Welfare. You can appoint an individual or an organisation, such as a trustee company, to make decisions about your property, but you can only appoint an individual to act as your personal care and welfare attorney.

When setting up a property EPA, you can choose when it takes effect and what powers you want to give your attorney: e.g., full control of your assets immediately if you want someone to manage your affairs; limited powers at a future date if you're going overseas; or only if you become mentally incapable.

A personal care and welfare EPA allows your attorney to make critical decisions about your care and welfare only in the event that you are mentally incapable.

An EPA can be set up by your lawyer or by a public trustee company like the Public Trust, Guardian Trust or Perpetual Trust. It's a good idea to set them up when you make your will.

Further information
www.publictrust.co.nz   www.perpetualtrust.co.nz
www.guardiantrust.co.nz

PROTECT YOUR ASSETS

On 1 February 2002, the Property (Relationships) Act 1976 was extended to cover de facto and same-sex relationships. In essence, people living in a de facto relationship, the definition of which is somewhat unclear, do not become subject to the Act until the relationship has lasted for a period exceeding three years. This is a very grey area because it's not clear how to determine exactly when a relationship started. For example, is it when you move in together, or is it when a more intimate relationship begins? With respect to married couples, the time spent in a de facto relationship is now taken into account when determining the length of the relationship.

Effectively what happens is that if you separate after being in a relationship for three years or more your assets will be split down the middle, unless there are extraordinary circumstances. The most common example of this is where one person has given up their career to care for children from the relationship, thereby enabling the other to advance their career. The carer might then get more (such as the house) to make up for loss of earning potential.

You can decide to opt out of the Act, subject to certain criteria. The way you do this is by signing a 'contracting-out' agreement, which basically states what belongs to each partner individually, and what are joint assets. Both parties must get independent legal advice, and the agreement must be in writing and witnessed by a lawyer, who certifies that the effect and implications of the agreement have been fully explained.

If you do have a contracting-out agreement, it's important to make sure it matches the wishes expressed in your will, any trusts you have, or any other asset-protection structures you have in place.

A discussion about how you will deal with your assets in the event of a relationship break-up can be one of the most difficult conversations you will have, but it is also one of the most important. When we go into a new relationship we imagine it's going to last forever, so it's very hard to talk about the practicalities of how to deal with money if the relationship does not work. However, if you don't address these issues and the relationship dissolves, it can be incredibly messy, time-consuming, stressful, and in some cases expensive, to sort out. If both partners enter into the relationship with similar amounts of assets it's not so important, but you still need to consider these issues. If you are not convinced of the importance of this, go and talk to a lawyer who specialises in this area — I am sure you will be well and truly convinced by the end of the conversation!

ENSURE BACK-UP: 1

None of us gets excited about the idea of insurance, but it can be one of the most important things to organise. Basically, insurance is a necessary evil, and unfortunately it's not something you can go out and buy when you need it. Insurance is about planning for the 'what ifs' in life before they happen.

The basis of insurance is that the insured passes risks that they are unable or not prepared to fund to the insurer, who covers the cost if a risk event occurs. Most people are pretty good at insuring their physical assets, typically referred to as 'general insurance'. Below is a brief overview of this type of insurance.

House insurance

There are two types of house insurance:

Insured value: this pays a specific amount based on the market value of your home at the time you take out the policy. It is the cheapest option, but it is not often used as it frequently doesn't cover the actual cost of rebuilding the property, or take into account any increase in the value of the property over time.

Replacement cover: this is worked out on the square metre size of your property (the building or 'improvements'), and will cover the cost of rebuilding the property regardless of the price. This is the cover most people use.

Contents insurance

This covers the contents of your home, and other belongings, while they are in your home or if you are temporarily in another part of the country. In the event of loss, in some cases you are paid the replacement value of the item (i.e. the cost of replacing it), while in others you are paid the indemnity or market value (i.e. what you would have got if the item had been sold). If you have expensive items like a camera or jewellery, you may want to itemise them on your policy.

Car insurance

You need car insurance to cover any damage to your car, and any damage you cause to someone else's car. There are two main types:

Third-party cover: this is the most basic insurance, therefore the cheapest, and it only covers you for damage you do to someone else's car.

Comprehensive cover: this covers any damage to your car as well as any damage you do to someone else's car.

Not all policies are the same — read the policy documents carefully so you know exactly what you are covered for.

ENSURE BACK-UP: 2

Quite apart from general insurance, it is important to think about the other types of risk you could face and the financial strain they could put on you and your family. You need to determine which risks you wish to transfer (i.e. insure against) and which you are comfortable self-insuring against (i.e. you are prepared to live with the consequences).

These types of insurance, which are generally called personal insurance, are outlined below. To help explain them, I have included an example for each type.

Life insurance

This is for when you depart this world too soon, and it takes the form of a lump sum that is payable to the beneficiary of the policy. This can be used for things like paying any debts, paying off your mortgage, funeral costs, the future education of your children, or to provide an income for your spouse and family. There are two main types of life insurance:

Endowment and whole-of-life policies: these have a savings component to them, so you pay higher premiums. I am not a big fan of this type of policy, because insurance and investment are two different things and I don't believe they work well in the same product.

Term life: this is simply a set amount of cover for a set time period. Because there is no investment component, the premiums are lower than for endowment policies.

Whole-of-life policies are often referred to as 'bundled' policies, and term life as 'unbundled' policies.

Salutary tale 1:

Geraldine, Simon and their three young children were living a comfortable life. They had a house they loved, Simon had a great job with a good salary, and Geraldine ran a part-time business from home. One day, when he was just 43, Simon had a sudden heart attack and died. They had life insurance, but unfortunately it was only just enough to cover the mortgage, and nothing else. Geraldine, already facing her own grief and looking after three small children who had just lost their father, suddenly found life was a real struggle financially. Unless she got her business running again the family would have no money to live on. She now regretted not taking the advice of their risk broker and increasing the amount of Simon's life insurance.

Income protection

Also known as disability insurance, this is one of the most important types of insurance as it enables you to insure one of your most valuable assets: your ability to earn an income. For example, if you earn $50,000 a year and are now aged 40, your future income can be roughly calculated at $1.25 million (25 years x $50,000). It is the potential loss of this income that an income protection policy insures. If you are unable to work as a result of an illness or injury you are paid a monthly income. You can choose a stand-down, or waiting, period of four, eight or 13 weeks before any income is paid. Under most income protection policies you are able to insure up to 75% of your taxable income.

Salutary Tale 2:

At 47, Claire thought she had it all — a high-powered career as a human resources consultant, and a young child she adored. However, she realised that as the sole income earner she needed some extra security in case she was unable to work. Just two years later, a mammogram revealed that Claire had cancer. Through her income protection policy she received a benefit of $3,200 a month, enough for her to stop worrying about money and concentrate on getting well.

Your ability to earn an income is one of the most valuable assets you have.

Total and permanent disablement

This type of insurance, which is usually not expensive, may pay you a lump sum if you become permanently disabled. There is usually a minimum six-month period before any payment is made, so the permanence of the disability can be verified.

Salutary Tale 3:

Geoff and Jane found that they got to the end of each month with just enough money to live on. Fortunately, now that their two children were at school Jane was able to work and provide much-needed income. They had sought advice from an insurance broker, who suggested a full protection plan. Although they agreed this would be a good idea, in the end they only took out a life insurance policy as it was the cheapest and that was where they thought their greatest risk was. Unfortunately Geoff became ill, and was confined to bed, unable to work. His company paid his wages for a couple of weeks but that was all they could afford and they had to let him go. Six months later Geoff's health had not improved and he was still confined to bed for most of the day. Had they taken out the policy their adviser had recommended, Geoff might have been entitled to a lump-sum payment from a total and permanent disablement policy.

Trauma protection

Sometimes referred to as serious illness cover, this provides a lump sum payment if you suffer a trauma or critical illness, like a heart attack, stroke or cancer. This is the sort of trauma that can result in a number of unforeseen expenses, such as the cost of medical treatment, rehabilitation (possibly including career retraining) and home help.

Salutary Tale 4:

John (57) had spent 15 years building up his very successful consultancy business. Now, with their two children grown up and independent, John and his wife were enjoying the freedom to pack up and go sailing whenever they wished. Then one day John suffered a stroke that incapacitated him and kept him off work — and the boat — for three months. Fortunately he had trauma protection cover, which paid a lump sum of $50,500. He also received income protection payments totalling $3,922 and a bed confinement payment of $227. With no financial stress, John could concentrate on getting well, and three months later he was back in business.

Medical insurance

At a time when the costs of medical care keep rising and hospital waiting lists keep growing, medical insurance is becoming more and more relevant. There are two main types of medical insurance: one covering hospitalisation and specialist care, the other a comprehensive cover that also includes doctors' and dentists' fees.

Salutary Tale 5:

Derrick, at 58, was a married father of three with a hectic lifestyle juggling family commitments and work as a store manager. Suddenly he suffered a heart attack, and everything changed. Not only did Derrick have to slow down, but he really needed an angioplasty — a procedure to reopen his blocked blood vessels. He could wait for treatment in a public hospital, or get it done privately — at a cost of $11,473. Because he had medical insurance he was able to have the procedure done privately, and almost immediately.

Don't focus too much on the cost of insurance — instead, look at its value to you while you build up your wealth and assets. I often find that people have insurance they don't necessarily need, but don't have the policies they do need. As a general rule of thumb, you don't need a lot of insurance when you are young — the key one is income insurance. When you have a family and are taking on debt you will need the most insurance. Then, as your children grow, your debt reduces and your assets increase, you may be able to decrease your cover.

BACK-UP FOR LESS

Tips for saving money on your insurance:

- Increase the level of your excess.

- You usually get a discount on home insurance if you have smoke and burglar alarms.

- A discount is usually given if you have all your insurances with one company.

- Pay your insurance annually. There is a premium of approximately 9% on your insurance if you pay monthly.

- Be careful when making a claim. Ensure that the amount you are paid is more than the cost of losing your no-claims bonus.

- Shop around — some companies offer discounts for particular categories or age groups. Better still, work with an insurance broker who understands the various options.

- Extend the waiting period on your income protection. Make sure you have an emergency account or funds readily available to cover you for this extended period.

DID YOU KNOW?

★ **On average we each have a one-in-eight chance of having a stroke in our lifetime.**
(Stroke Foundation of New Zealand, 2004)

★ **About 80% of all cancers are thought to be related to lifestyle and environmental factors.**
(Cancer Society of New Zealand, 2003)

★ **One in seven New Zealanders will die during their working lives.**
(Statistics New Zealand, Demographic Trends, 2001)

★ **In 2000, the major cause of death was cancer, followed by heart disease.**
(Mortality & Demographic Data, New Zealand Health Service, 2000)

★ **The leading causes of death between the ages of 15 and 24 were external causes such as accidents, violence and poisoning.**
(NZ Age Specific Death Rates 2000–2002, Statistics New Zealand, 2002)

★ **30–40% of all amputations are performed on patients with diabetes.**
(www.vascular.co.nz, 2004)

★ **The leading cause of disability is a disease or illness (40%), followed by accident or injury (30%).**
(Statistics New Zealand)

★ **Three-quarters of all claims for work-related injuries in 2003 were made by males.**
(Injury Statistics, Work-related Claims, ACC New Zealand, 2003)

FIND A BUNKER

For most people, their home is the most significant asset they will ever own. Not only does owning your home provide you with shelter, it also provides a compulsory form of saving through your mortgage repayments.

In the last 20 years or so, home ownership levels in New Zealand have dropped from around 75% to close to 67%. Statistically speaking that is quite a significant drop. In addition, the evidence suggests that the number of New Zealanders who own their homes is continuing to decline.

There are probably a number of reasons for this. We live in a more transient society than formerly — people move around a lot more with their jobs, they are getting married later, and they want more flexibility in their living arrangements. There also doesn't seem to be as much emphasis on the importance of having your own home, and long-term renting is becoming increasingly common.

One worrying reason is that it is becoming increasingly difficult for people to be able to afford to buy a home — first, saving for the deposit, and then meeting the mortgage repayments, especially in the major cities and more desirable areas. Over the last couple of decades the cost of housing has increased from 60% of our income to 130%. That obviously means it is much more challenging for today's first-home buyers than it was for their parents' generation.

HOUSING MATTERS

Let's look at an example. You purchase a home for $250,000, with a $50,000 deposit and a mortgage of $200,000 over 25 years. Assuming an interest rate of 8%, your monthly repayments would be $1,543. In 25 years, assuming an average capital growth rate of 5%, your home will be worth $870,322.

Now before you fall off your chair, note that we are talking 25 years, and that inflation will account for approximately half this increase in value (assuming inflation averages 2.5% over the long term).

Saving and renting versus buying

If you decided to rent long term and put your money into savings, to be in the same place financially as buying a home:

- You would need to pay your weekly rent

- And save $1,500 each month for 25 years, assuming 5% annual growth — without missing one payment.

This would give you a total of $902,208, similar to the amount of value you would have in a home.

AN ALTERNATIVE TRENCH

In a small number of cases people may be financially better off renting than buying their own home, provided they invest regularly and accumulate an amount similar to the value of a freehold home in, say, 25 years' time. But most people don't have the discipline to do this, and are therefore better off buying a house and paying off the mortgage. Of course the other advantages of having your own home are that you have security — there's no risk of the landlord asking you to leave at the end of a tenancy — and you are able to add value to the house over time.

For more detailed information on buying vs renting read *Buying a Home Isn' t Everything: How Renting Can Work for You* by Paul and Stella Winstanley (New Holland Publishers). It's a thorough look at the topic.

DIG IN

Saving for a house deposit is tough not just because the cost of housing has increased, but because there is so much competition for our money. Many people simply decide that getting the latest flat-screen TV or a really nice car is more important than putting their money away to save for a house deposit. A generation or two ago there was very little consumer finance available, so you had to save up for things and buy them when you had the cash. And there wasn't so much pressure from advertising, making us believe we have to have things now (remember Battleplan 45 about keeping up with the Joneses?).

If you really want to buy your own home you need to be staunch. So, how do you start saving for the deposit?

How much do I need?

You need to look towards saving between 5% and 20% of the value of the house you want to buy.

Value of house	5%	10%	15%	20%
$250,000	12,500	25,000	37,500	50,000
$300,000	15,000	30,000	45,000	60,000
$350,000	17,500	35,000	52,500	70,000
$400,000	20,000	40,000	60,000	80,000

Ideally you want to save as much as you can, for two reasons. First, to make it easier to borrow: the bigger your deposit, the lower the risk to the bank, meaning they are more likely to lend to you. Second, the bigger the deposit, the lower the mortgage, and the easier the repayments will be.

How do I save?

The secret, of course, is simple — start now. The first thing to do is to work out when you want to buy the house, and how much you need for a deposit. For example, if you want to buy a house worth $300,000, and are aiming for a minimum of 10%, then you will need $30,000. If your timeframe is two and a half years then you will need to save $1,000 each month in order to reach your target. You will get some interest on your savings, and you can use this extra money to pay for legal fees, valuation, moving costs, etc.

The best way to save this money is to put aside a small amount from each pay cheque. Go back to Battleplan 12, where I talk about creating a spending plan, and make a house-deposit account part of your system. So your get-ahead account may become your house-deposit account until you have saved enough for your deposit. An automatic payment to this account is by far the best way of doing this, as you don't have to think about it.

If you work through this process you will develop a great savings habit, and you will soon see the pay-off. It may be hard going in the beginning but you will be surprised how your money will grow over time.

Where should I save?

The key thing here is to use a low-risk savings vehicle. For example, you are not likely to use the sharemarket for this. The sharemarket can be volatile and unless you really know what you are doing, or have a longer timeframe, say a minimum of five years, it's best to stay away from it when saving for your house deposit. The best options are:

High-interest savings account at a bank. Typically you need to have a minimum balance of say $5,000 to get the higher interest rates, and there will often be a small fee if you drop below this amount or make withdrawals. These accounts have great flexibility, however, as you can put money in whenever you like, easily set up an automatic payment, and you can take money out when you like. Of course you won't be doing this until you are ready to buy your house!

Term deposit. These pay a higher interest rate than a savings account but you can't take the money out until the end of the term, which can range from 30 days to five years. You also can't save into them on a regular basis. However, you could save into your savings account and every so often transfer the money to a term deposit with a timeframe to match when you think you want to buy your house.

Cash management trust. These are provided by banks and fund management companies, and are essentially a managed fund which holds a range of fixed-interest investments. They are based on a unit price basis, are also pretty flexible, and often pay more than a bank account.

Whatever account you choose, its sole purpose should be for your house deposit. It's best to put aside your savings and forget about them until you need the money, otherwise you may be tempted to use it for other things. Before you make your decision, consider:

- the interest you will earn

- how long you are committing your money for, and how easy it will be to access

- the level of charges.

The important thing is to find a savings option that best suits your needs. The one with the highest interest rate may not necessarily be the best option for you. If you are unsure about the differences between the various accounts on offer, talk to your bank.

SECURE THE GROUND

Buying a home not only provides security in the form of somewhere to live, but paying off the mortgage is also a great form of compulsory saving. However, it is also one of the biggest financial decisions you will ever make, so it is important to get it right. Here are some tips.

1. How much can you borrow? Your bank or mortgage broker will be able to tell you this. Be careful not to borrow so much that you don't have anything left in your budget after making your mortgage payments.

2. Have a look at how different interest rates will affect your repayments. For example, if you are buying at the low end of an interest-rate cycle, at around 6.5–7%, see if you can afford the repayments at the high end, when they could be 8.5–9%. A lot of people have had big shocks lately when renewing their fixed-rate mortgages and have been really struggling to afford the higher repayments.

3. Consider which area you want to live in. Do you want to be close to work, family and friends, good schools, shops, etc?

4. What type of home do you want? An apartment, villa, townhouse? Old or new? How many bedrooms? Small or large section?

5. How does what you want stack up against what you can afford? You may need to make some compromises.

6. Do your market research. Work with real estate agents but also do your own homework and get to know the market in the areas you are considering. When it comes to putting in an offer you will be well-informed about how much you should be paying for the property.

7. Get your lawyer involved before you finalise the sale and purchase agreement to ensure it has the correct conditions and clauses.

8. Remember that real estate agents are salespeople. Some are very knowledgeable, but many have only been in real estate a short time and have very little expertise.

9. As part of your due diligence get a valuation and building inspection, and a LIM report (a Land Information Memorandum, from the council) to make sure you know what you are buying. Getting these reports done should be conditions in your sale and purchase agreement.

10. Put some thought into the type of mortgage that best suits your circumstances (see Battleplan 70).

11. Carry out a pre-settlement inspection to make sure that everything you thought was included as part of the deal is still there. If there is a problem your lawyer can hold some settlement money back until all the issues are resolved.

12. If you are planning to renovate do a detailed budget of the costs, then double it (that's typically what I have seen happen). Make sure you can afford it, and that the work will be worth it to you.

Apart from the actual cost of the house, you will need to pay a number of other fees, such as:

* Legal conveyancing fees of $800–1,500, depending on how complex the mortgage is.
* The bank's loan administration fee, around $500; however, you can often negotiate the removal of this fee.
* Low-equity fee (see Battleplan 71).
* House valuation, $400–500 depending on the value of the house.
* Building inspection report, $500–1,000.
* LIM report, $150–400 depending on the council.
* Connection fees for the phone, power, TV, etc.
* House and contents insurance.
* Moving costs, approximately $100 per hour.
* Mortgage repayment insurance, to cover your repayments in case of death or major illness.

Stephen Hart, the author of *Where to Live in Auckland* and co-presenter of TV2's *House Calls*, has written an excellent book called *The Streetwise Home Buyer: The Step by Step Guide to Smart Home Buying in New Zealand*, which will take you through the process of buying a home. See www.wheretoliveinauckland.co.nz

CONSOLIDATE YOUR ATTACK

Now you're starting to see how you really can win the money war, it's time to have another look at the basics of saving so you can continue to meet your goals. Here are six essential Battleplans for saving.

SAVINGS AND INVESTMENTS

THE FIRST STEP IN A SUCCESSFUL SAVINGS PROGRAMME IS TO COMMIT TODAY TO MAKING SMALL, REGULAR SACRIFICES. IF YOU SAVED $20 A WEEK FOR 30 YEARS, AND EARNED 5% NETT PER YEAR, YOUR TOTAL SAVINGS AND INTEREST WOULD BE WORTH $73,000! COMMITTING TO A REGULAR SAVINGS PLAN AND TAKING ADVANTAGE OF COMPOUNDING INTEREST CAN PRODUCE AMAZING RESULTS.

IF YOU HAVE A **SPECIFIC SAVINGS GOAL** YOU CAN EASILY WORK OUT HOW MUCH YOU NEED TO SAVE EACH WEEK TO MAKE IT HAPPEN. ALWAYS USE A **SAVINGS OR INVESTMENT ACCOUNT** THAT'S SEPARATE FROM YOUR EVERYDAY ACCOUNT, SO YOU WON'T BE TEMPTED TO SPEND THE MONEY.

SAVING MONEY IS A STATE OF MIND. BEFORE YOU START, YOU HAVE TO **STOP BELIEVING YOU ACTUALLY NEED ALL THE STUFF YOU'VE BEEN SPENDING MONEY ON.** SURE YOU WANT IT, BUT THAT'S NO EXCUSE FOR BUYING IT. THE NEXT TIME YOU SEE SOMETHING YOU WANT TO BUY, TAKE THE $50 OR $100 IT WOULD COST OUT OF YOUR WALLET AND STASH IT SOMEWHERE. SEE?

YOU ONLY GET TO SPEND EACH DOLLAR ONCE, SO YOU WANT TO MAKE SURE YOU GET THE **BEST VALUE OUT OF THAT DOLLAR.** BECOME FRUGAL. WHEN YOU ARE ABOUT TO BUY SOMETHING, ASK YOURSELF IF YOU REALLY NEED IT, OR WOULD YOU JUST LIKE TO HAVE IT? OFTEN YOU FIND IT IS JUST A WANT, RATHER THAN A **NEED.**

SET THAT **SAVINGS TARGET** AND START PUTTING YOUR MONEY ASIDE REGULARLY EACH WEEK OR MONTH. IT WON'T BE LONG BEFORE YOU FIND THAT YOUR $300 HAS GROWN TO $3,000, AND YOUR $3,000 TO $30,000, AND YOUR $30,000 TO . . .

ONCE YOU'VE STARTED, MAKE SURE YOU KEEP THE **BALL ROLLING.** HOW DO YOU DO THAT? NO BIG SECRET THERE — YOU PUT AWAY SMALL AMOUNTS OF MONEY AS **REGULARLY** AS YOU CAN, AND YOU KEEP DOING IT. MOST PEOPLE MISTAKENLY BELIEVE THAT FANCY INVESTING TECHNIQUES OR PICKING THE RIGHT SHARE OR PROPERTY ARE WHAT GET RESULTS. IF THERE IS A SECRET, IT'S **CONSISTENCY** AND **TIME.**

FINANCE THE CAMPAIGN

One of the most frequently asked questions is whether you should pay off your mortgage before you start investing. Even the experts don't agree on this, with some people for the idea and others against it. I think it depends, which is not an overly helpful answer, so let's look at why.

From a purely financial perspective you are usually better to pay your mortgage off before you start a savings or investment programme. This is because you pay your mortgage with money you earn after tax. Therefore, to be better off financially by investing you would need to earn a return of around 10–11% gross per annum (the equivalent of about 7–8% after tax, which is probably what you are paying on your mortgage). There are not many investments that will produce this level of return unless you take on a reasonable amount of risk, and know what you are doing.

However, the fact is that people rarely do anything for purely financial reasons —our emotions, desires, level of discipline and all sorts of other factors come into play. In my experience people tend to pay off their mortgages within the same timeframe regardless of whether they are putting additional money aside for investment or not.

Generally, I recommend that, if you can afford it, you pay off your mortgage faster than the standard 25-year term, and also contribute to a regular savings or investment plan. One of the positives about starting an investment plan while you still have a mortgage is that you get into the habit of saving, which is a really useful discipline that will help you achieve your financial goals.

One of the concerns I have about waiting until you have paid off the mortgage is that New Zealanders have a habit of trading up their houses as they can afford it. This can mean that they don't pay off their mortgages until much later in life, which can mean they start saving too late.

So while in most cases it may be better financially to pay off your mortgage before you start investing, in reality this might not be the best overall option. It's about what *you will do*, not what *you can do*! From a holistic perspective most people are going to be far better off if they do both.

SURVEY THE FIELD

Once you get the basics sorted out, your financial future is largely dependent on putting together an investment strategy. Before you start there are a number of things to think about. How much do you want to invest? For how long? What are your expectations? How do you feel about risk? What are your financial goals? Where do you see yourself in 10, 20 or 30 years? The answers to these questions will dictate the sort of investment portfolio you have.

It's important to decide how active you want to be as an investor. Many people want the higher returns that come from active investing, but they aren't prepared to put in the necessary time to become skilled, or they can't tolerate the level of risk that often comes with more active investing and higher returns.

The following Battleplans cover some of the things you need to consider.

SAVING IS A SHORT-TERM THING: YOU MIGHT SAVE FOR A NEW CAR, A HOLIDAY, A HOUSE DEPOSIT, ETC. INVESTING IS FOR THE LONG TERM, OFTEN WITH THE IDEA OF BENEFITING FROM THE RETURNS IN YOUR RETIREMENT YEARS.

HISTORY HAS SHOWN US TWO THINGS. FIRST, THE NATURE OF INVESTING IS CYCLICAL — MARKETS MOVE UP AND DOWN, AND INDIVIDUAL MARKETS MOVE AT DIFFERENT TIMES AND DIFFERENT RATES. SECOND, IN INVESTING, **RISK AND RETURN ARE STRONGLY LINKED.** GENERALLY SPEAKING, THE HIGHER THE RETURN, THE HIGHER THE LEVEL OF RISK.

UNLESS YOU ARE AN EXPERT IN YOUR CHOSEN AREA OF INVESTMENT, **DON'T KEEP ALL YOUR EGGS IN ONE BASKET,** NO MATTER HOW ATTRACTIVE OR SAFE THAT BASKET LOOKS! **SPREADING YOUR INVESTMENTS** ACROSS A DIVERSE RANGE OF ASSETS, MARKETS, INDUSTRIES, COUNTRIES, FUND MANAGERS AND INVESTMENT STYLES PUTS YOU IN A GOOD POSITION.

INVESTORS OFTEN MAKE LONG-TERM DECISIONS BASED ON SHORT-TERM EVENTS. IT'S HUMAN NATURE TO WANT TO GET OUT WHEN THE GOING GETS TOUGH, BUT SELLING WHEN YOUR INVESTMENTS AREN'T WORTH AS MUCH AS YOU'D LIKE IS SIMILAR TO SELLING A HOUSE BECAUSE THE PROPERTY MARKET IS DOWN. TO GET THE BEST OUT OF YOUR INVESTMENT, YOU NEED TO BE IN IT FOR THE LONG HAUL.

IF YOU **INVEST A SET AMOUNT REGULARLY** IN A MANAGED FUND, FOR EXAMPLE, YOU WILL GET MORE UNITS WHEN THE PRICE IS LOW AND FEWER WHEN THE PRICE IS HIGH. OVER THE LONGER TERM, THIS MEANS THE OVERALL COST OF YOUR UNITS AVERAGES OUT AT A LOWER PRICE. THIS IS A **GREAT STRATEGY** FOR **PASSIVE INVESTORS.**

ALL SUCCESSFUL INVESTORS USE EXPERTS TO HELP THEM MAKE THE BEST FINANCIAL DECISIONS.

YOUR KEY ALLY

The power of compounding is possibly the most underrated concept when investing. Compounding is earning interest on interest, something Einstein described as the 'greatest force in the universe', the 'eighth wonder of the world'. In simple terms, compounding is about reinvesting all the interest or profit you receive on an investment, as opposed to putting it into your current account and spending it.

The best way to make the most of compounding is to start early. The earlier you start investing, the more years you earn interest, and as a consequence the larger the investment base and the interest on it becomes, thereby giving you a higher return. This can be seen in the table opposite, which shows how much the growth tends to accelerate over time. Look at how much the investment grows over the first 10 years compared to the second 10 years — in the second 10 years the growth is around three times that of the first 10 years.

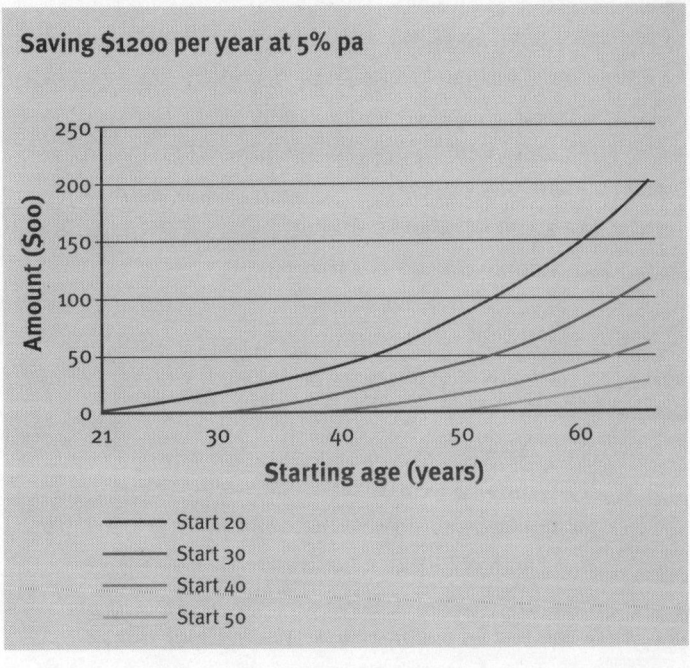

Saving $1200 per year at 5% pa

The benefits of compounding don't show overnight, so you need to have patience. The key thing is to hang on. Often when you are starting out it doesn't seem as if you are making a lot of progress, but if you keep on investing the returns really start to accelerate. The beneficial effect of compounding (effectively, earning interest on your interest) is only felt through reinvesting that interest. Over 20 years the difference in the value of a portfolio where the income has been reinvested rather than taken out is extraordinary.

The 'Rule of 72' says that if you divide the number 72 by an investment's annual rate of return after tax (i.e. the nett return) you will get the number of years it will take the investment to double in value. How does that work?

- If you stash $5,000 in an investment that returns an annualised 5%, your $5,000 will turn into $10,000 in 14.4 years (72 divided by five).

- If you put $5,000 in an investment that earns an annualised return of 10%, your $5,000 will be worth $10,000 in just 7.2 years (72 divided by 10).

CALLING IN EXTRA TROOPS

Shares can be key investments, but they can be daunting for a beginner. There are several ways to get started.

- Use a stockbroker.

- Do the research yourself and buy using an internet account.

- Use a software package and become a trader.

- Buy 'bundles' of shares through one of the NZX's (NZ Stock Exchange) products.

- Buy managed funds, which will include a number of different shares.

- Put a portfolio together with a financial adviser.

Like any market, the sharemarket has cycles: periods of strong growth, periods of no growth, and even some with negative growth. You need to invest over a timeframe of five to 10 years — if you are a passive investor, the longer the better.

You also need to think about how much time you want to spend on your investing. Generally, the more time you put in the better the returns. If you want to spend limited time you are probably better off using a managed fund or professional advice.

The first thing you need to do, however, is some homework, so you understand the options available to you. There are lots of books on investing in the sharemarket (many of which will be available at your local library). One I like is *Shares: Seven Ways to Beat the Market* by Martin Hawes; it's full of useful information for both novices and long-term investors.

Some community colleges have introductory courses on investing, many of them run by very experienced tutors who work in the field and like to teach. Check your local paper for courses, and use the internet. Before enrolling always check who is running the course: often the cheaper ones are trying to sell you something. Most importantly, be thorough in your research and get good advice.

Further Information
www.sharechat.co.nz has a daily sharemarket newsletter that you can subscribe to free
www.fundsource.co.nz a New Zealand research company
www.goodreturns.co.nz a general investment website
www.morningstar.net.nz a New Zealand research company

SECURE MORE TERRITORY

If you are considering investing in property there are a number of choices, including residential, commercial (retail, office and industrial) and forestry. You can either invest directly, or through a listed property trust or unit trust, both of which are vehicles that have a collection of properties. I cover the basics of investing directly into residential property below.

There are a number of reasons for New Zealanders' well-known 'love affair' with property as an investment.

- Until about the 1980s there were few investment options in New Zealand compared with other western countries. (For instance, in Europe the first managed funds were available around the end of the 18th century.)

- There have been some good tax advantages to investing in property that weren't available for other types of investment, although these have reduced with recent tax changes.

- Property investors have traditionally used leverage much more than in business or the sharemarket. (In Australia it is very common to leverage into shares.) See the Glossary for a brief explanation of leverage.

- And, of course, we are a nation of DIY lovers.
  Many people like the hands-on nature of property
  investment; for example, around 25% of Kiwis use
  professional property managers, whereas the figure in
  Australia is around 80%.

Property can be a fantastic investment but, like any other,
you need to put some time and effort into it. Here are some
Battleplans you need to consider:

HAVE A PLAN

- Are you looking for capital growth, cashflow or a combination of the two?

- What type of property do you want to buy?

- Do you want a place you can add value to?

- Do you want to be an active or passive investor?

- What is your timeframe? Ideally you should hold an investment property for a minimum of 10 years.

BEFORE INVESTING IN PROPERTY, TAKE A LOOK AT YOUR **FINANCIAL POSITION.** BANKS GENERALLY TAKE A LONG-TERM VIEW IN RELATION TO PROPERTY INVESTMENT. THEY CONSIDER ALL ASPECTS OF A FINANCE APPLICATION, INCLUDING FOCUSING ON DEBT LEVELS AND **YOUR ABILITY TO SERVICE DEBT** (YOUR INCOME LEVEL) IF FACTORS CHANGE.

IT'S IMPORTANT TO UNDERSTAND HOW THE NUMBERS STACK UP. MAKE SURE YOU ARE **REALISTIC** ABOUT WHAT RENT YOU ARE EXPECTING. **FACTOR IN ALL THE EXPENSES** YOU MAY INCUR, LIKE REPAIRS AND MAINTENANCE, BODY CORPORATE FEES, WATER AND PROPERTY RATES, INSURANCE, PERIODS OF VACANCY AND OF COURSE INTEREST COSTS.

YOUR CHOICE OF PROPERTY TYPE WILL DEPEND ON YOUR **PERSONAL PREFERENCES,** THE **TYPE OF STRATEGY** YOU HAVE, AND WHETHER YOU ARE AN **ACTIVE** OR A **PASSIVE** INVESTOR. NEW PROPERTIES ARE OFTEN VERY ATTRACTIVE TO LONG-TERM AND MORE PASSIVE INVESTORS. MAKE SURE YOU BUY FROM A QUALITY DEVELOPER IN A GOOD GROWTH AREA.

SOME AREAS OF NEW ZEALAND ARE LIKELY TO DO BETTER THAN OTHERS. TYPICALLY, THE LARGER THE CITY OR THE CLOSER THE CITY CENTRE, THE **LOWER THE YIELD** AND THE HIGHER THE POTENTIAL FOR **CAPITAL GROWTH.** THERE ARE A NUMBER OF REASONS FOR THIS. IN CONTRAST, THE SUBURBS AND SMALLER CITIES TEND TO HAVE HIGHER YIELDS BUT LOWER CAPITAL GROWTH.

UNLESS YOU PLAN TO BECOME AN EXPERT, YOU SHOULD EMPLOY ONE TO DEAL WITH TENANTS. IF YOU ARE NOT PREPARED TO LEARN ABOUT THE WORKINGS OF THE RESIDENTIAL TENANCIES ACT AND MANAGE YOUR PROPERTY CLOSELY, IT'S BEST TO USE A PROFESSIONAL PROPERTY MANAGER.

GET GOOD ADVICE: YOUR TEAM MAY INCLUDE, AMONG OTHERS, A LAWYER, ACCOUNTANT, VALUER, FINANCIAL ADVISER, BUILDING INSPECTOR, PROPERTY MANAGER AND MORTGAGE BROKER.

Further information

The following all provide advice and information for property investors or potential investors:

www.nzpif.org.nz (New Zealand Property Investors' Federation)
www.propertytalk.com
www.landlords.co.nz
www.qvinsider.co.nz
New Zealand Property Investor magazine
The Complete Guide to Residential Property Investment in New Zealand by Andrew King and Lisa Dudson

ACT LIKE A GENERAL

There are approximately 500,000 businesses operating in New Zealand. Most have fewer than 10 employees, and many only have one or two. We have one of the highest rates of business ownership per capita in the entire world.

Many Kiwis dream of having their own business and becoming their own boss. It can be a great way to get ahead financially, but it can also be a lot of hard work, and the buck stops with you! The decision to have your own business should not be taken lightly, as 75% of businesses fail in the first four years.

So how do you decide if you want to have your own business?

Advantages

- You are your own boss

- You decide when and how much you want to work

- You control the income you make

- You can make big profits

- You can leverage your time

- There can be tax advantages

- Flexibility

- The opportunity to work from home

Disadvantages

- Clients often dictate how you operate

- You will probably need to work 60–80 hours per week for the first few years

- It can be lonely and worrying

- Lots of paperwork

- It is common to make a loss in the first year or two

- You could get ripped off

- Legal liability issues

DEVELOP YOUR STRATEGY

You need to either come up with a good idea or buy into an existing business. Buying into an existing business may involve less risk, but it will probably require more money. Whichever way you decide to go, you will need to do some research to make sure there is a market for your idea and, most importantly, that you can make money from it. I have seen lots of great ideas in business, but having an idea and making a decent living out of it are two different things.

PROFILE YOUR SKILLS

The next thing you need to work out is what skills you have and how they fit with your proposed business idea. Personality or wealth profiles can be useful tools to help you establish what your strengths and weaknesses are. Usually when you start a business you have to do everything, but it is important that the key part of your business is aligned with your main strengths.

WRITE A BUSINESS PLAN

Far too few people write a business and marketing plan before they launch into business. The old saying, 'If you don't know where you are going any path will get you there' is very true; if you don't know where you are going, how do you know whether you are on the right path, or know when you get to where you want to be? You don't need to write *War and Peace*, but you do need to cover the key areas of your business. Your plan should include things like:

- concept or idea

- branding and marketing

- key relationships, customers, strategic alliances

- cashflow and funding

- resources needed (staff, technology, stock)

- your team (lawyer, accountant, financial adviser, business mentor, bank manager).

KEEP MOTIVATED

Having your own business requires a lot of self-motivation and discipline. Some things are going to work and some are not. You need to be totally focused and passionate about what you are doing so that you can work through the inevitable tough times.

While having your own business can be extremely rewarding, it does demand perseverance. In my experience, people who start their own business tend to work twice as hard in the first few years and make half as much money as they did in their previous job. However, if you stick with it and love what you do the rewards will come.

Further information
www.smallbusinessexpo.co.nz run in Auckland, Wellington and Christchurch between April and June each year
www.biz.org.nz a government website with a vast amount of information and resources
www.businessmentor.org.nz free business mentors for people who have been in business more than six months
www.homebizbus.co.nz resources for people who run a home-based business

EXTEND THE SUPPLY LINE

As you continue to manage your finances successfully, don't forget to investigate how the government can help you. As part of the Working for Families package, families with children 18 years or under may be entitled to assistance from Work and Income New Zealand (WINZ) and the Inland Revenue Department (IRD).

Family assistance

Family assistance is made up of four types of payment: Family Support, In-work Payment, Family Tax Credit and Parental Tax Credit. You may qualify for more than one form of assistance. What you are eligible for depends on:

- the number of dependent children under your care and their ages

- your family income

- where your income comes from, e.g. salary or wages

- any shared childcare arrangements that are in place.

Affordable Housing Supplement

This is an accommodation supplement that is delivered by WINZ. Depending on where you live, your income, your assets and your housing costs, you may qualify for assistance with your rent, board, mortgage or other essential housing costs.

Childcare subsidy and OSCAR (Out of School Care and Recreation) subsidy

These two childcare subsidies are also delivered through WINZ. The childcare subsidy is for children under five (or under six if you receive a Child Disability Allowance), and provides for up to 50 hours of childcare a week while parents are working. The Out of School Care and Recreation (OSCAR) subsidy is for children between 5 and 13, and provides for up to 20 hours a week of before- and after-school care, and up to 50 hours a week of care during the school holidays.

Free early childhood education

On 1 July 2007 the government introduced up to 20 hours of free early childhood education for three- and four-year-olds, for teacher-led early childhood education services. For information, check out the Ministry of Education website, which includes a list of contact numbers for the ministry's regional offices, **www.minedu.govt.nz**.

Where to from here?

Other useful sources of information about family assistance are the Working for Families website **www.workingforfamilies.govt.nz** and the IRD website **www.ird.govt.nz** (or you can phone the department on 0800 257 777).

For information on the Affordable Housing Supplement, Childcare subsidy or OSCAR you can go to the WINZ website **www.workandincome.govt.nz** or phone them on 0800 774 004.

www.teamup.co.nz is another useful website, which was set up to provide easy access to information about education.

LEAVE THE FIELD OF ENGAGEMENT

Why do we retire at 65? In fact, the retirement age is quite arbitrary. When the world's first state pension was introduced in Germany in 1880 (at a time when the average life expectancy was just 45), the age of entitlement was in fact 70; it was lowered to 65 in 1916.

In just a few decades, the number of years you are likely to live in retirement has doubled. If you had retired during the 1970s you could expect about 10 years in retirement before you passed away in your mid-seventies. People retiring today are likely to spend between 20 and 25 years in retirement. For those whose retirement is a long way off, the length of time spent in retirement is anyone's guess. The only certainty is that it will be longer than today.

How much do you need?

This obviously depends on your lifestyle. Some people think you need 70% of your current income when you retire, while others think you need 100%. I believe the reason for this range is the changing style of retirement — formerly it was seen as a more sedate time of life, whereas today people enjoy much better health after 65 and are far more active than previously. Generally this means they will require more income.

As a guide to how much you might need, multiply your

LOOKING TO THE FUTURE

current income (or the income you think you will want when you retire) by 20.

For example:

You would like $25,000 per annum nett income by the time you retire, on top of the New Zealand superannuation.

$25,000 x 20 = $500,000

This means that over your working life you will need to accumulate investments or savings totalling $500,000.

Another way to approach it is to divide your current savings by 20. So, if you currently have savings of $400,000:

$400,000 ÷ 20 = $20,000

Thus your $400,000 will give you an income of $20,000 per year.

Note that these are approximate figures, and are based on a 5% nett return on your investments. Your capital will reduce in value over a 30-year period, and inflation also needs to be taken into account, depending on how far away retirement is for you.

Current after-tax rates of New Zealand Superannuation

The New Zealand Super rates aren't flash, and if this is your only source of income it won't allow you to live very comfortably.

Rates at 1 April 2007

Fortnightly payments	Before tax	After tax (where there is no other income)
Single (living alone)	$673.30	$554.12
Single (sharing)	$619.32	$511.48
Married, de facto or civil union couple (partner not included)	$511.40	$426.24
Married, de facto or civil union couple (both partners qualify)	$511.40 each	$426.24 each
Married, de facto or civil union couple (only one partner qualifies)*	$486.56 each	$ 406.44 each

* This amount may be affected by other income you receive. People whose payments started before October 1991 may get more than this. See **www.workandincome.govt.nz** for further information.

As the number of elderly people increases worldwide, all countries are struggling to work out how they are going to support an aging population in the future. This is one of the main reasons New Zealand's KiwiSaver scheme was introduced (see Battleplan 114). In my opinion, it's highly likely that the age of entitlement to New Zealand Superannuation will be raised toward 70 before too long. This means you will need a lot more money for your retirement if you don't want your standard of living to deteriorate.

Many people think of retirement as so far away they don't need to think about it yet. However, it's important to start planning for your retirement financially as soon as you can.

DID YOU KNOW?

* By 2051 there will be 300,000 women and 200,000 men over 80 years of age in New Zealand.
* Approximately 63% of people over the age of 65 earn less than $15,000 a year.

CALLING UP THE KIWI

KiwiSaver is a voluntary, work-based savings plan run by the government and the IRD (Inland Revenue Department) which started on 1 July 2007. It is designed to make saving easier, and to help people maintain a long-term savings habit.

How does it work?

If you start a new job, or decide to opt in, 4% of your total pay (before tax) will be deducted from your salary and put into your KiwiSaver account. Total pay includes bonuses, overtime and commissions. You can increase the amount to 8%, and you can change between these rates at any time.

Your employer will provide you with information on joining KiwiSaver. If you start a new job you will be enrolled automatically, but you can tell your employer you don't wish to participate in the scheme. You have from day 14 to day 56 from the day you start your new job to decide if you want to opt out.

If you are a non-employed adult you can join on your own by simply contacting a KiwiSaver provider.

What are the benefits?

- The government provides your first $1,000 (tax free) when you join the scheme.

- If you are 18 or over you'll get a tax credit matching the contribution you have made, up to a maximum of $20 per week ($1042.86 per year). This money is paid into your KiwiSaver account annually. You have to live in New Zealand to get this tax credit (though there are some exceptions). If you leave New Zealand permanently and withdraw your KiwiSaver contributions this tax credit amount is repaid to the government.

- The government will contribute $40 per year ($20 paid twice each year) to offset your investment management fees, which are already discounted.

- From April 2008, your employer has to add to your contributions to KiwiSaver, starting at a minimum of 1% of your pay, and increasing by 1% each year until it reaches 4% in April 2011. Your employer may contribute more than this amount, and they can also start before April 2008.

- Employer contributions will be tax-free up to a limit of 4% of your before-tax pay. Employers will also receive a subsidy from the government of up to $20 per week to help with their contributions.

- There is a potential tax saving — all KiwiSaver schemes have to be PIE (Portfolio Investment Entity) compliant which means the maximum tax you will pay from 1 April 2008 is 30% or 19.5% if that is your marginal tax rate. This is of benefit if you are in a 33% or 39% tax bracket.

- The government may give you another $1,000 for every year you contribute to KiwiSaver (with a minimum of three years or $3,000; maximum five years or $5,000) towards a deposit for your first home. This will depend on your household income and the price of the home.

- When you buy your first home you can make a one-off withdrawal of all your KiwiSaver contributions and earnings (including any employer contributions) except the original $1,000 'kick start' and all government contributions.

- After you have been in KiwiSaver for 12 months you may be able to split your contributions, with up to half going toward repaying your mortgage and the rest to your KiwiSaver savings. This only applies to existing mortgages on your own home (i.e. not an investment or holiday home). Your tax credits and any contributions your employer makes cannot be diverted to your mortgage.

Can I access my money?

In general, not until you are 65 (the current age of entitlement) or have been in the scheme for five years, whichever is the later. However, there are some exceptions, such as:

- You can make a one-off withdrawal to help you buy your first home, after you have been with KiwiSaver for three years.

- In cases of significant financial hardship.

- If you suffer a serious illness.

- If you move overseas permanently, after having contributed to KiwiSaver for 12 months or more.

Can I stop at any time?

After you have been in KiwiSaver for a minimum of 12 months you can apply for a contributions holiday of between three months and five years. You can do this as many times as you like.

Where is my money invested?

You can choose a scheme provider, or if you haven't done this by October 2007 IRD will automatically allocate you one of six default providers. These default providers each have a default fund where a minimum 75% of the total is kept in cash and fixed-interest investments, and less than 25% in growth funds (such as shares). At the time of writing there are about 30 approved providers which you can choose from, and many have more than one fund (allowing you to choose the level of risk).

What happens if I want to change the KiwiSaver scheme I am in?

It's very simple to change the scheme you are in. You just complete a transfer form provided by your current scheme provider, and an application form for the scheme you wish to transfer to.

What happens if I change jobs or leave the workforce?

Your KiwiSaver account will go with you.

How does it affect employers?

Starting on 1 April 2008, employers must contribute 1% of your pay per year, rising by 1% per year to a maximum of 4%. To help with this, the government will make employer contributions tax-free to a maximum of 4% if matched by the employee, and contribute up to $1,042.86 per year to the employer (provided this is matched by the employee).

How does it work if I am a beneficiary, a mother or don't work?

As long as you are a New Zealand resident and are under 65 you can join. My recommendation is to contribute the minimum of $20 per week if you can afford it, and the government will match this. If you do go back into the workforce, you can increase your contributions at that point.

How does it work if I am a temporary or casual employee?

Temporary employees will be automatically enrolled if their employment is longer than 28 days; for casual agricultural workers this period is three months. Your employer is responsible for deciding if automatic enrolment applies to you. At the end of the working period you can either continue to contribute independently or wait until you start a new job.

How does it work if I own my own company?

If you own your own company and pay yourself a salary using PAYE, then you should be able to get both the employee contribution from the government and the employer contribution, subject to the various guidelines outlined here. It's best to get advice from your accountant.

How does it work if I am self-employed, a sole trader or in a partnership?

You can join a KiwiSaver scheme and receive all the benefits of the scheme, but you will only be entitled to the employee contribution from the government, as essentially you don't have an employer.

Should I pay off my debts before I start KiwiSaver?

Some people believe it is best to pay off any debts (excluding your mortgage) before investing in KiwiSaver. I don't necessarily agree, because I doubt people will pay their debt faster if they don't contribute to KiwiSaver.

What happens if I go overseas in six months, or before the end of the KiwiSaver tax credit year?

Your government credit will be proportionate to how much of the year, from 1 July to 30 June each year, you are a member. You need to work out what you are entitled to, based on when you joined KiwiSaver, and how much you have contributed during that time.

How is my KiwiSaver fund paid when I reach 65 and am eligible to receive it?

You will have a choice of either taking it as a lump sum or receiving income from it, similar to current superannuation policies.

What is the latest age I can enrol in KiwiSaver?

As long as you are a New Zealand resident and are under 65 you can join. If you decide to join at 64 you can. The government will contribute $1,040 per year for a maximum of five years provided you also make the minimum contribution of $1,040 per year. You don't have to contribute for five years, although it would make sense, as you effectively double your money for five years because of the government's contribution.

Should I enrol my children?

You can enrol your children (i.e. those under 18) in the scheme. You would need to set up a relationship directly with one of the providers and contribute at least the minimum amount (for example, for the ING scheme this is $400 per year). People under 18 don't receive matching contributions from the government, but they do get the $1,000 kickstart, and the $40 per year administration fee, and it is a great way to encourage young people to save (remember the old Post Office Savings Bank accounts?). They won't be able to access the funds until they reach 65, but they may be eligible for the government housing subsidy of $3,000 after three years or $5,000 after five years of contributing, at either age 18 or when they start working (plus they can withdraw their contributions as a deposit on a first home).

Is my KiwiSaver account part of matrimonial property in the event of divorce or de facto separation?

The current understanding is that it will become part of matrimonial property, therefore falling under the Matrimonial and Property Act, and will be taken into account in the event of separation.

What happens to my KiwiSaver money if I die before I use it all up?

Your KiwiSaver money is your personal money so it will be paid out to your estate.

How does it work if my company already has a superannuation scheme to which both I and my employer contribute?

This is a bit of a grey area. Some employers with existing policies have applied to get their scheme KiwiSaver approved. The challenge is that it must have all the features of KiwiSaver. Currently most employer superannuation schemes enable the employee to take their money when they leave their job and/or receive it when they are 55, which doesn't meet the KiwiSaver guidelines. Another issue is that any existing employer superannuation scheme to which the employer contributes is part of an employment contract and KiwiSaver is a government scheme, therefore the theory is that KiwiSaver will need to be on top of the existing superannuation for current employees, unless the employer can change its scheme to be KiwiSaver-approved. Some employers are changing their employment contracts so that their employees can choose whether they go into the current employer scheme or into KiwiSaver, or choose to do both. Some may put all new employees into KiwiSaver and not the employer scheme.

What if my employer does not contribute?

If you are a member of an employer scheme where your employer does not contribute you will most likely find that KiwiSaver is a better option for you. This is simply because with the government $1,000 kickstart and its annual contribution of $1,042.86 to your scheme (provided you also contribute a minimum of $1,040) the overall return on investment is higher effectively because of this 'free' money that the government adds. It also pays $40 towards the cost of fund fees. In most cases it will make sense for you to either stop contributing to your current scheme or do both.

What should I do if I already have my own personal superannuation fund?

You can participate in KiwiSaver as well or make a decision on which you choose.

Can you contribute separately to KiwiSaver?

If you are an employee the only way you can contribute to KiwiSaver is through your employer, paying a minimum of 4% of your salary or wages into the scheme.

What if I change jobs?

Because KiwiSaver is linked to your IRD number, your account will be changed to your new employer when you change jobs.

Should I change to a company structure if I am a sole trader or have a partnership?

There are many factors to consider in setting up a company structure, quite apart from any KiwiSaver benefits. I strongly recommend you get advice from your accountant.

Should I contribute 4% or 8%?

Most commentators recommend that you only contribute 4%.
If you can afford 8%, I suggest you take advice from a qualified
financial adviser so that you consider all your options.

Is joining KiwiSaver a good idea?

Absolutely. The government and employer contributions
make KiwiSaver a very attractive savings option. The biggest
challenges of long-term saving are getting started and
maintaining the habit of saving consistently. KiwiSaver has been
designed to make this easy.

How much is it going to cost me and what will I get?

Example: If you're 25 years old

Annual pay ($)	Weekly pay ($)	4% weekly contribution ($)	By 65 you'll save* ($)	8% weekly contribution ($)	By 65 you'll save* ($)
20,000	385	15	183,286	31	254,504
30,000	577	23	252,125	46	355,263
40,000	769	31	318,505	62	456,023
50,000	962	38	384,885	77	556,782
60,000	1,154	46	451,265	92	657,542
100,000	1,923	77	716,785	154	1,060,580

* Includes government incentives and employer contributions as set at June 2007. Note, these figures are rounded to the nearest year and don't take into account the fact that you may be investing for a part-year.

Example: If you're 45 years old

Annual pay ($)	Weekly pay ($)	4% weekly contribution ($)	By 65 you'll save* ($)	8% weekly contribution ($)	By 65 you'll save* ($)
20,000	385	15	65,531	31	90,258
30,000	577	23	88,793	46	123,612
40,000	769	31	110,540	62	156,966
50,000	962	38	132,287	77	190,320
60,000	1,154	46	154,035	92	223,674
100,000	1,923	77	241,024	154	357,089

* Includes government incentives and employer contributions as set at June 2007. Note, figures rounded, as on previous page.

Further information

www.kiwisaver.govt.nz the official KiwiSaver website

www.ird.govt.nz to order the IRD booklet Your Introduction to KiwiSaver

www.sorted.org.nz provides a KiwiSaver calculator

www.hnzc.govt.nz included details on the housing eligibility criteria

RECRUITING NEW TROOPS

Once you have more money to work with, you may want to start thinking about putting some aside to fund your children's education. This is a crucial investment that potentially delivers outstanding returns, not all of which can be readily calculated in dollar terms.

It's often our own level of education that dictates how much we earn, how we live, the quality and fulfilment we enjoy in our lives, and the sort of expectations we pass on to our children. However, these days education doesn't come cheap.

A recent study showed that in New Zealand students from schools in affluent communities are nearly five times more likely to attend university than those from poor areas. And those students who do go on to university now have to cope with the issue of substantial student fees. A significant number of students now leave tertiary education with some level of student debt. Some say the system is creating an entire generation of educated people steeped in debt — and that's before they get a mortgage. Others say the system is causing people to leave the country for better-paying jobs elsewhere, or to delay decisions about starting a family.

As a parent, what is the best way to deal with this financial challenge and help your children fund their tertiary education? As with any savings, the key to success is deciding on your goal and starting early. Below are some examples of how much you would save by setting aside the same amount over various timeframes.

Timeframe (years)	Amount per month	Rate of return	Total
10	$100	3%	$14,144
15	$100	3%	$22,910
20	$100	3%	$33,094

Note: I have used a conservative 3% rate of return to allow for inflation, i.e. to take into account the fact that the money you save will buy less in the future than it would buy today.

As with all savings, taking a long-term approach lessens the monthly burden and allows the power of compound interest to start working in your favour. Put the funds aside in a separate account so they don't get used for other things. For example:

- *Bank account.* This will provide the lowest return, but is ideal when you are starting to save.

- Unit trust. You would probably look at a balanced growth fund, and you would typically use this option if you were starting the fund five to ten years before you needed it. This timeframe would allow for market fluctuations.

- *Education funds specifically designed for this purpose.* There are a few options available. One I would not recommend is the ASG fund; I find this fund difficult to understand, and it has too many restrictions.

It is worth getting advice on the most appropriate option, as you want to make sure the funds can be used for something else (such as put toward a house deposit) if your children decide not to go on to tertiary education. An education fund can also be a great gift from a grandparent, or members of a family could pool together and each contribute a small amount. What better payout could there be for everyone than having a family member who has been helped to get the education they need to reach their potential, and to be able to start their working life without the shadow of a student loan hanging over them?

SPREAD THE WORD

Knowing how to manage money is one of the most important skills you can pass on to your children. You don't need to be a financial whiz to be able to teach them the basics. Here's how you can help your children to learn basic money management.

1. **Use pocket money.** Pocket-money day is a perfect opportunity to teach your kids some real money skills. Rather than seeing it as a payment for good behaviour, or for doing jobs around the house, try using pocket money to teach your children about saving, spending and making money grow.

2. **Encourage your kids to save for things they want.** Have your children divide what money they receive between jars for long-term savings, short-term savings, money to spend and money to give away. They can then watch the contents of the jars grow. Alternatively, open a bank account for them. This way they learn that material goods don't come free, and that there's a trade-off between spending money now and saving it to buy something later.

3. **Use everyday encounters to help kids learn about money.** Don't be shy about discussing your budget with your children. Show them the household bills, the withdrawals on your ATM receipts, or your bank statements.

4. **Explain interest.** Your kids need to learn that they earn interest on money saved but must pay interest on money borrowed. Having a bank account lets them see what interest they have accrued on their savings — or you could pay them interest on money saved at home.

5. **Be aware of money personalities.** Are your children savers or spenders? Knowing this will help you learn how to help them, so have them complete the Kids & Money Quiz in the Kids & Money section on **www. sorted.org.nz.**

6. **Talk about money with your children.** It's from discussions about how much money you make, what that needs to be spent on, and why they can't always have just what they want that children learn about the value of money.

7. **Be consistent.** When you have made a rule or an agreement about money with your kids, keep to it! Don't give in and buy that toy — kids need to learn that when money's gone, it's gone.

8. **Keep records.** Encourage account-keeping by having your kids keep written accounts of deposits, withdrawals and interest. Or choose a bank account that has a passbook.

9. **Find out what's happening at school.** Schools also have a role in helping kids learn about money. Ask what they have already been taught, so you can build on that.

The Retirement Commission is lobbying for money management to be taught at school, but it may take some time for it to become a compulsory subject so it's important that you teach your children money skills. In the future they are likely to face student loans, hire purchase, credit card bills and mortgages. Right now they can be learning that there's a trade-off between what they spend today and what they save for tomorrow. Saving today reduces your choices right now, but it increases your choices in the future; borrowing creates choices too, but you have to pay the money back, plus interest.

Further information

- There is a whole section on **www.sorted.org.nz** to help you teach your kids about money. There are interactive online games, a money personality quiz, and a heap of other stuff designed to make learning about money easy and fun. The tips above are sourced from this site.
- Suzanna Stuart, an Auckland-based adviser, has written two excellent books about children and money: *Start Talking Cents* (Random House) and *Your Family Fortune* (Random House).

WHEN THE STRATEGY FAILS

You may have to face the fact that in the short term you may not be able to overcome your mountain of debt. Is bankruptcy an option?

On 3 December 2007 the Insolvency Act 1967 was replaced by the Insolvency Act 2006, which takes account of changes such as the much greater use of credit today than in the past. Under the Act there are three options available to you if you are having trouble paying your debts:

1. Summary Instalment Order
2. No Asset Procedure
3. Bankruptcy.

1. Summary Instalment Order

This can be put in place if you owe less than $40,000. It is designed for situations where you have some means of repaying your debts, but are struggling to repay them all. A repayment programme is arranged with your creditors and formalised. A percentage of your debts may be written off, depending on your ability to repay what you owe.

MORE TO THINK ABOUT

2. No Asset Procedure

This is aimed at debtors who are on a low income and have no means of repaying their debts. You will be eligible for this if:

- you have no realisable assets

- you have not previously been through a No Asset Procedure

- you have not previously been bankrupt

- your total debts are between $1,000 and $40,000

- you don't have the means to repay any of your debts.

You will still be responsible for any fines, child support payments and student loans, but any other debts will be written off.

3. Bankruptcy

Bankruptcy is the most onerous of the three options. It is a legal process that enables you to get relief from the debts you cannot repay, although it does not cover all of your debts. You will still be liable for:

- all payments ordered by the courts, such as fines or reparation (compensation) payments

- maintenance and child support payments

- any advances or overpayments you have received from WINZ

- any debts you incur after the date of your bankruptcy.

If you go bankrupt an Official Assignee will be appointed to take control of your assets. You must disclose all of your assets to the assignee, who will decide which you may keep and which will be sold to pay off your debts. You are entitled to keep cash up to $400, tools of your trade to the value of $500, and furniture and personal effects to the combined value of $2,000.

What other options do I have?

Before you decide if bankruptcy is the best option for you, there are a number of steps you can take:

- Sell your possessions. Decide what you don't really need and sell it.

- Cut your spending. See Battleplans 26–43.

- Get budgeting advice. A budget adviser will help you work out a plan to limit your spending and help you pay off your debts (see Battleplan 12 for how to create a budget).

- Consider whether debt consolidation is a good option.

- Try to reach an agreement with your creditors. Most will be helpful, and work out a realistic payment plan if you genuinely want to make it work.

- Try and get another job to increase your income. Check out the other ideas in Battleplans 15–24.

Bankruptcy should always be considered a last resort. We all have an obligation to make every effort to repay our debts. Before any of the options above are applied you will need to go through a very comprehensive assessment process to see if you qualify. If you are earning a good income you will have to continue to pay off your debts. The level of payments will be worked out at the time of application.

Although bankruptcy lasts for three years, your credit record will be affected for up to seven years. Your credit history may also be available in other countries, as many of the credit agencies have international affiliations.

Don't ignore your creditors, they won't go away. If you feel you are drowning in debt, take action and get some help.

For more information visit **www.insolvency.govt.nz** or **www.familybudgeting.org.nz**.

DID YOU KNOW?

★ In 2007 bankruptcies increased by 20% compared to the previous year.

PEACETIME CELEBRATIONS

Although Christmas can be the happiest of times, when we have our loved ones around us, for many people it is the most financially stressful. So how to prepare for it?

Start early, by putting together a Christmas budget. Let's look at the types of things it should include:

- Make a list of all the people you need to buy gifts for. Set a limit to how much you want to spend on each one, and a limit for the total. Start buying gifts early in the year when you can get things on sale. Can you make your own cards, and gifts such as baking, preserves, handcrafts, etc?

- Are you going on holiday? If so, how much will it cost? As well as accommodation and travel costs, don't forget to include spending money.

- Plan for Christmas Day. Are people coming to your place? If so, how many? Think about the menu and estimate how much it will cost for food and drinks. What should you ask other people to bring? If you are going to someone else's place, what do you need to take with you and how much will that cost? If you are going to a restaurant, what is the price per person?

- How much extra do you need to plan for during the holiday period? This is often a time of higher spending on food and alcohol.

- What about decorations — are you going to buy a Christmas tree? Do you have enough decorations left over from last year? Boxing Day sales are a great time to buy really cheap Christmas cards, wrapping and decorations. If you have children, making decorations is a great way to save money and get everyone into the Christmas spirit.

Write down all the things you need to buy, and put an amount next to each one. Once you know the total amount you can start planning. And once you have made your plan, do your best to stick to it. Most people just 'wing' it, put everything on their credit card, then get stressed in January because they haven't thought about how to pay for it all.

Go back to the spending plan exercise in Battleplan 12. If you think Christmas might be difficult for you, put it into your budget today and put a little money aside throughout the year.

CALL IN MILITARY ADVISERS

A doctor looks after your physical health, a dentist your teeth, a lawyer your legal needs and a counsellor your relationship. But who cares for your financial health?

You can decide to do this yourself, in which case you need to become knowledgeable about financial matters, or perhaps it's time to consider using an adviser to help you achieve your financial goals. We know that not all advisers are created equal, so how do you find the best one for your needs?

You can start by asking friends and colleagues for recommendations, but you should also do your own homework. You will probably be working with your financial adviser for a number of years, so you need to find someone you can trust and feel comfortable with. Use the following questions to help you; they can be applied to any adviser, including a financial adviser, accountant, lawyer or mortgage broker.

Questions to ask potential advisers:

- What qualifications do you hold?

- What is your role in the company, and who owns it?

- How long have you been involved in this field?

- What practical and professional experience do you have?

- What industry bodies or associations do you belong to?

- What do you charge for an initial consultation?

- What are your other services and their associated fees?

- What types of services am I entitled to if I become a client of your company?

- How do you handle client money? Do you use a trust account?

- Do you have professional indemnity insurance?

Once you have this information you can make an informed decision. Remember to take all these factors into account, not just the size of the fees.

Tips for getting the most out of an adviser:

- Make sure you feel comfortable with your adviser.

- Be open and honest with them. Anything you tell them is in confidence, and the more they know the better they can advise you.

- Decide what outcomes you want to achieve.

- Give feedback — your adviser is not a mind-reader.

- Be realistic. No matter how good your adviser is, it is not likely they will be able to sort out all your issues in an hour or two. They should be able to give you a good start though, depending on the complexity of your situation.

Once again, I cannot overstate the importance of getting help from someone who knows what they are doing. The most financially successful people have very well-qualified teams of experts around them who play a significant part in their success. I am not suggesting you need a huge team to help you, but whether you are planning your long-term financial goals, looking for a way to reduce your debt, or starting a business, the advice and skills of an expert can be invaluable. The reality is that you are unlikely to have all the skills you need, so get some help.

The industry body for financial advisers is the Institute of Financial Advisers (IFA). Their website **www.ifa.org.nz** has some useful information, including a list of members.

DID YOU KNOW?

★ 65% of New Zealanders get their financial advice from friends and family.

★ A similar percentage of people earn less than $15,000 after the age of 65 — so is this a good place to get advice?

THE ULTIMATE PRIZE

Now you've got your debt under control and are saving, it's time to think about really big goals. How do you become wealthy?

In an American study of saving behaviour by economists Steven Venti of Dartmouth and David Wise of Harvard, more than 75% of respondents said they knew their retirement savings were insufficient. While that's shocking, even more remarkable is their discovery that how much you save has very little to do with how much you earn. Venti and Wise divided the 7,700 households they studied into 10 income groups. They found that the top 10% of the lowest income group had saved more than $150,000 per household. Meanwhile, middle-income folks, on average, had only $45,000 in assets. A similar study in New Zealand would yield very similar results.

Key findings of the study of saving behaviour

- There's a huge variation in wealth at every income level: many low-income families have almost nothing, but the same is true of many high-income families.

- Income alone doesn't explain wealth disparities. Some of the lowest-earning households had managed to accumulate significant wealth.

- Income differences explain just 5% of the disparities.

- What the researchers called 'chance events' — inheritances, medical bills, marital status, number of children — explained about 4% of the disparities.

- Investment choices explained about 8% of the variations.

- In other words, the vast majority of the differences in wealth had nothing to do with income, chance events or investment choices.

- What did explain most of the differences in household wealth? Venti and Wise concluded it was this: how much the families chose to save. Those who made it a priority to save built wealth, regardless of their income level, individual circumstances or choice of investments.

This research clearly shows there is no excuse for not saving. What Venti and Wise found to be the most significant savings factor was no more jaw-dropping than this: Ya just gotta save it!

So how can you save when you barely live on what you earn?

Saving is a two-step process. First you retrain your brain, then you find all kinds of clever ways to live on less.

REVIEW THE TROOPS

Just as you take your car to the garage once or twice a year to have a check-up and get a new warrant, you also need to do a regular check-up on your finances. Money doesn't manage itself, and your finances need to be monitored and reviewed on a regular basis. If you have developed good systems this review should be relatively painless and take very little time.

Many people's idea of a financial review is to see if they have enough money in their bank account to get them through to the next payday. Since you've got this far in the book, you won't be in this category!

Your financial review should include the following:

- Have you managed to pay off all your consumer debt?

- How much has your nett worth improved?

- How much do you still owe on your mortgage? Can you pay more off it?

- Have you got the correct mortgage structure for your current situation?

- Are your insurances up to date?

- Is your estate planning up to date? Is your will current?

- Do you know where you are spending your money?

- Is your budget/spending system working effectively?

- Are all your important documents filed correctly? Do your executors, trustees, etc. know where they are?

- How are you tracking your progress toward providing for your retirement?

- Have you set new goals for the coming year?

After your review, don't forget to take some action.

VICTORY!

Well done! You have made it through to the end. By now you should feel confident about being a good money manager, and your finances will be in much better shape than when you started. You are well on the way to winning the money war and you are no longer reeling from incoming sniper action. The enemy's guns are silent and you have things under control.

This is what you have achieved:

- You understand the basics of money management.

- You have created some good habits that will continue throughout your lifetime.

- You know how to control your spending.

- You have a straightforward budgeting system that takes very little time to manage, and it works.

- You don't feel stressed about money.

- You understand the importance of keeping on track, and regularly reviewing and monitoring your progress.

- You feel comfortable when making financial decisions.

- You know how to get help.

- You have a positive attitude toward money, and understand that this is crucial to becoming financially successful.

So much to celebrate! Now that you have developed these skills, you can carry them with you through the rest of your life and never be stressed about money again. Even if a war broke out again you would know how to fight back. You would pick yourself up and carry on. What you can never lose are the inner resources that lead to success.

CODE OF PERSISTENCE

This code was written by Harold Sherman, author of *How to Turn Failure into Success*.* Commit it to memory and use it to motivate yourself to become more persistent.

- ★ I will never give up so long as I know I am right.
- ★ I will believe that all things will work out for me if I hang on to the end.
- ★ I will be courageous and undismayed in the face of poor odds.
- ★ I will not permit anyone to intimidate me or deter me from my goals.
- ★ I will fight back to overcome all physical handicaps and setbacks.
- ★ I will try again and again and yet again to accomplish what I desire.
- ★ I will take new faith and resolution from the knowledge that all successful men and women have had to fight defeat and adversity.
- ★ I will never surrender to discouragement or despair no matter what seeming obstacles may confront me.

*First published in 1982 by Prentice Hall.

THE END

Or is it really the beginning? The beginning of a life free of money stress and full of financial success? Your attitude — not your intelligence, talent, education, technical ability, opportunities, or even hard work — is the main factor that will determine whether you will live your dream. If you believe you have a great relationship with money, you will develop the financial habits you need to have abundant financial health.

I wish you all the best, and am fully confident that you are more than capable of developing the financial habits that will ensure you have the money you need to live the life you want.

Lisa

As a seasoned veteran of the money wars, these Battleplans have worked for me, and I know they'll work for you. So stick to your guns!

The Money Man

CASE STUDIES

The following case studies are taken from Cream Media's television series *Money Man*. The participants were questioned three to four months after filming to see how their situations had changed.

SERIES 2, EPISODE 6: MICHELE

Age	42
Assets	
• Home	$350,000
• Car	$3,000
• Business interests (stock)	$80,000
• Managed funds	$3,500
Total	**$436,500**
Debts	
• Home	$310,000
• Credit card	$9,500
• HP	$5,000
Total	**$324,500**
Savings before the show	$0
Savings after the show	$13,500
Debt before the show	$324,500
Debt after the show	$310,000
Home owner	Yes

Financial improvements

At the time of the show, Michele had taken out an additional mortgage of about $70,000, so her total mortgage was around $310,000. She had her house revalued and it came in at around $375,000, so she borrowed a further $35,000 to pay for some marketing initiatives for her business. The total mortgage was then $345,000.

Several months after the show, she had repaid the $35,000 and some of her floating mortgage, so the mortgage was down to $299,950. She says she may draw on some of this to do further marketing, although she has had a couple of enquiries from potential investors and may look at that option first (however, as she is a self-described 'control freak', that's a tough one!).

Michele has cleared her credit cards, which were about $9,500, and she has kept one, with a $2,500 limit, which she pays off each month.

She also now has savings of $13,500, which she is keeping in a separate bank account. As her mortgages are on fixed interest, and most are at less than the 8.2% she is earning on her savings, it is not worth repaying them at this time. However, she aims to use this account to pay each of the fixed mortgages as they come off term over the next two to three years. After that her goal is to start putting away money for her retirement, and a three-day working week.

Michele still has hire purchase payments for her carpet, which is $213.11 per month, with 16 months to go ($3,409.76). Again, it is not worth paying it off early as the interest of 7% is less than she is earning on her savings account, and the HP isn't structured to give her much saving on the interest if she repaid it early.

Questions and answers: Michele

What were the reasons you decided to go on the show?

I had always been a chronic shopper, and was constantly living beyond my means, deep in debt and just scraping by each month. I had started a new business and kept the same lifestyle, so I just wasn't coping with the additional mortgage I had taken out and was also not focused on the business. I was heading towards complete disaster, and the sick feeling in my stomach before each payday, when I realised I was getting deeper into debt, was becoming incredibly stressful. My 'shopping addiction' was no longer amusing; it was becoming seriously concerning. So when I was offered the opportunity to go on the show, I thought I would probably get something out of it, so I grabbed it!

How were you feeling about your financial position at the time?

I was concerned, but I still had a very blasé attitude towards it — 'She'll be right' or 'Here for a good time, not a long time, so who cares?' However, the mounting debt was beginning to make me feel physically sick and out of control which is not something I am comfortable with!

How has your life changed since being on the show?

I no longer shop at random; I don't buy food that I don't eat. I am very focused on my business. I feel much stronger and more accountable for my own actions. I feel like I have a responsibility to take better care of both myself and my finances. I now find it easy to walk away from things that I don't absolutely need. With every cent I could potentially spend, I think first — how could I promote my business with this money instead, or could this go into the account to clear the mortgage?

What did you find the most difficult about the tasks the show gave you?

The most difficult thing was learning to say no to 'things', and to people who had been very used to me saying 'yes' to every party and every social outing. Not giving things away, such as discounting my product, or letting people not pay for things. Not being the one to shout the tickets, or buy the dinner.

What did you find the easiest?

To draw the cash out each week and just live on that. This was possibly helped by the fact that I didn't have a lot of time to shop because, once I saw where I was at, and had such a focus on where I needed to get to, it was so easy to stretch that money out and not feel bad about not buying rubbish. I think seeing half the contents removed from my wardrobe and realising how much that didn't actually hurt made me realise just how little connection I actually had to this 'stuff' that I had spent so much time and money accumulating.

What were the most important things you learnt, and why?

The show was an incredible wake-up call to just how much money I had literally burnt on superfluous rubbish that wasn't making me any happier. I realised how gullible I had been to retail advertising. Now I don't read junk mail, I hardly watch TV (and avoid ads like the plague), and when I see those signs 'two for the price of one' I know it's a con, and I just think 'I'm so on to you, but I'm not sucked in any more' — and boy, do I enjoy walking away!

It made me realise that my business had potential and I had to step up to the plate and make it happen.

I learnt that I shopped out of complete boredom or to seek relaxation, but that it was empty satisfaction — the buzz I get now out of seeing my business growing (i.e., credits showing on the bank statement instead of debits) is extraordinary!

It made me very comfortable to make the statement 'I hate cooking' and for that to actually be okay! I think I always felt that was some sort of failing, so I bought all this food in the

hope that one day I would be a 'better' person. I now have no
issue with the fact that I REALLY hate to cook. It's something
everyone else needs to get the hell over. For me, 20 minutes
spent cooking is 20 minutes when I could be reading — and
there is no comparison for me. Now I can hunt out healthy and
cheap 'ready-made' options, I am very happy with my choice.
I learnt to value my time. Working full-time and actively running
the business is very challenging, so when I do have time to
myself, the last place I want to be is in a shopping mall — I
need to really relax, and that means reading a book, writing, or
spending time with friends.

Most importantly, I learnt to value myself — discounting
my product is like discounting my own efforts, and I won't do
that. Saying no to other people is actually about taking care of
myself and my finances, rather than always putting their needs
first, and I love that liberation! Having Lisa Dudson acknowledge
that my ideas were good (in my business plan), and feeling so
comfortable doing the programme and being really open and
honest and getting great feedback from it, gave me the courage
to really put myself out there with my product, such as doing
other TV advertising, radio crossovers at shows, and selling face
to face. It gave me the confidence that I didn't have before.

How do you feel about your financial position now?

Incredibly proud, relieved and determined to make it even
better!

During the show I actually got another mortgage so I had
some money to pay for some marketing. Since then I have
turned over nearly $100,000 in sales, and have repaid my
floating mortgage. I have cleared all my credit card debt. I'm

possibly the only company in the country that does this — but I pay every single bill ON TIME (which was something I was always determined to do) and I never book any advertising unless I already have the money in the bank to pay for it. As my floating mortgage is now repaid, and the rest is fixed, I have a savings account that I put profits or any savings into each month, and the aim is to have enough in there by June 2008 to pay off the next chunk of fixed mortgage.

Knowing that I actually have a positive bank balance and that I can meet my financial commitments is an incredible relief. So my stress doesn't come from 'How can I pay for this?' but ' How can I find the time to do this as well?'

I'm also very happy about the fact that I am no longer dependent on income from a flatmate. That's something that I am feeling very empowered about.

The only other thing I feel I'd like to add is that I just wish I had done this 15 years ago. The experience has been one of the best things I have done in my life, and I can only imagine where I would be now if I had taken all this stuff on board and practised it that much earlier!

So, thanks to everyone for getting me here at last!!!

SERIES 2, EPISODE 2: DAVID & JO

Ages	
David	44
Jo	36
Assets	
• Car	$3,000
Total	**$3,000**
Debts	
• Credit card	$7,596
• HP	$3,028
• Student loans	$26,242
• Bank overdraft	$750
Total	**$37,616**
Savings before the show	$1,200
Savings after the show	$0
Debt before the show	$37,616
Debt after the show	$36,5790
Home owner	No

Financial improvements

Jo and David have paid off their Westpac overdraft, one of their GE Finance HPs (for kitchenware) and half their cellphone HP (before it incurred any interest). They are yet to make payments towards their computer HP. They are also making their monthly Visa repayments, however because one of their animals had to have surgery their credit card is still sitting at $8,000.

Questions and answers: David

What were the reasons you decided to go on the show?

My wife Jo and I realised we couldn't go on the way we were, and needed to do something radical about our finances. We had already lost thousands and didn't want to see that happen again.

How were you feeling about your financial position at the time?

It was going downhill fast and we were never going to get out of the traps we were in without help. We were spending more than we earned, and that led us deeper into debt.

How has your life changed since being on the show?

It has changed for the better. We now have our eyes open in terms of finance and realise that we can control it, and that impacts on how we feel, which then positively affects other areas of our lives.

What did you find the most difficult about the tasks the show gave you?

The most difficult task was sticking to our tight budget. I didn't see instant results, so for the first six weeks it was hard. But then we turned a corner when the budget caught up with us, and for the first time we had the money on hand for the electricity, which was great.

What did you find the easiest?

Doing the filming and just having fun with Brendon Johnson and the crew. We actually missed the excitement of having the crew around once they'd left.

What were the most important things you learnt, and why?

First and foremost, that we can come out the other end because we now have a plan. It will take a while, but as they say: 'Good things take time.' And secondly that you need to understand the hidden costs behind 'interest-free', etc. It's okay to buy things as long as you pay them off BEFORE the interest hits.

How do you feel about your financial position now?

I feel much better about my financial position. We lost about four months of debt repayment due to unforeseen things but that's okay because we still have a plan and we are still working towards it. I've had to readjust our budget a bit, but again that's all part of it and making sure our spending is within our income. I don't say we get it right all the time, more that we are now generally heading in the right direction.

Questions and answers: Jo

What were the reasons you decided to go on the show?

My husband David and I were getting further and further into debt.

We saw the Money Man *advertisement and joked about it. But then we decided that we needed something extreme and this could be it. So we put our names forward and the rest, as they say, is history.*

How were you feeling about your financial position at the time?

I was overwhelmed and had not paid attention to our finances for quite some time. I didn't like where we were heading but I didn't know how to get our finances back on track.

How has your life changed since being on the show?

Apart from our new-found fame in our neighbourhood and with our families, my life has changed with regard to the way we handle our finances. I no longer have my head in the sand, but know what we have and what we need to be doing with it. I feel in control of our finances and I love watching our debts decline.

What did you find the most difficult about the tasks the show gave you?

Making us run with the ball of debt round our ankles was the hardest task. Exercise is not normally in our daily plan.

What did you find the easiest?

Working with the crew and the production team was so much fun. When we started Money Man *we thought we were in for a rough time and a whole lot of humiliation, but everyone was great. Brendon is a big teddy bear!*

What were the most important things you learnt, and why?

We learnt to be realistic about our finances. We learnt what kind of budget we needed. It was like we were lost and then someone lit up a neon sign to tell us where to go. We learnt that a plan and discipline go hand in hand.

How do you feel about your financial position now?

I feel we are in control of our finances. We are on track, our bills are decreasing and getting crossed off. We know how to work our finances, what we have to do and when to do it.

We are very grateful to Money Man *and everybody involved in the process.*

SERIES 2, EPISODE 7: SCOTT & KATE

Ages	
Scott	24
Kate	23
Assets	
• Car	$14,500
Total	**$14,500**
Debts	
• Credit card	$2,028
• Student loans	$35,000
• Family loans	$400
Total	**$37,428**
Savings before the show	$1,000
Savings after the show	$0
Debt before the show	$37,428
Debt after the show	$24,000
Home owner	No

Financial improvements

Since the show, Scott and Kate have separated, and only Kate answered our questions. For health reasons she has had to leave her university study, and she is working part-time for a law firm.

Questions and answers: Kate

What were the reasons you decided to go on the show?

To seek help with setting a budget and getting my partner to see that I wasn't over-reacting to the financial situation we were in, and that we were in over our heads.

How were you feeling about your financial position at the time?

Very stressed and worried.

How has your life changed since being on the show?

I work out a budget and stick to it — I know where my money is going, and what I have to spend. Plus, the other half, who was so atrocious with money, is now gone, so there is money to spare without it being spent frivolously just because it's there.

What did you find the most difficult about the tasks the show gave you?

I didn't really find them that difficult at all. The challenges were great as they forced me to do something about managing my money.

What did you find the easiest?

Setting up a budget, once I knew how to do it. What we had to spend was there in black and white, which made it easier to stick to.

What were the most important things you learnt, and why?

How to budget! It helps to be able to see what is coming in and what is going out, and when you might have more expenses coming in than you originally thought.

How do you feel about your financial position now?

Great — or I will do once I start my new permanent job! I am planning to save enough for a deposit on a house/unit/flat within the next 18 months. I have no debt, only the usual phone/ power bills, and have regular savings set up.

SERIES 2, EPISODE 4: NICK & DEBBIE

Ages	
Nick	30
Debbie	48
Assets	
• Car	$13,000
Total	**$13,000**
Debts	
• Credit card	$750
• Car loans	$8,000
• Student loans	$500
• Personal loan	$9,500
Total	**$18,750**
Savings before the show	$0
Savings after the show	$1,000
Debt before the show	$18,750
Debt after the show	$17,500
Home owner	No

Financial improvements

In the three months since the show Nick and Debbie have managed to pay off Debbie's student loan and their credit cards, and have saved $1,000.

Their goal is to be completely debt-free in a year, and to save around $6,000 to pay for their wedding. Nick says they never want to borrow any money again!

Questions and answers: Nick

What were the reasons you decided to go on the show?

I earned a lot of money yet I had nothing to show as I lived a very lavish lifestyle.

How were you feeling about your financial position at the time?

Not the best; we were only managing to scrape through each month.

How has your life changed since being on the show?

Life has changed drastically for Debs and me. We now spend a lot of time cooking together and planning next week's meals, week in and week out. It's also a great feeling to know we are finally saving money.

What did you find the most difficult about the tasks the show gave you?

The most difficult task was shaving off my hair (although it was my choice).

What did you find the easiest?

Getting on with the crew, Brendon and all you ladies in the background — you were all fantastic!

What were the most important things you learnt, and why?

I learnt that money is a precious commodity not to be squandered — and that our cooking is a lot better than any takeaways.

How do you feel about your financial position now?

'Fan-flipping-tastic!' I feel like we are on our way to financial independence.

SERIES 1, EPISODE 2: NICOLE & ZALMAN

Ages	
Nicole	32
Zalman	33
Assets	
• Home	$230,000
• Cars	$10,500
• Savings	$1,000
Total	**$241,500**
Debts	
• Mortgage	$180,000
• Credit cards	$4,779
• Personal loans	$1,400
• Car loan	$10,000
• IRD	$6,000
Total	**$202,179**
Savings before the show	$1,000
Savings after the show	$5,000
Debt before the show	$202,179
Debt after the show	$220,000
Home owner	Yes

Financial improvement

Nicole and Zalman have paid off all their debt apart from the mortgage, and they have also had a second baby. They have started building an extension on their house and have landscaped the front garden. In order to pay for this they borrowed an extra $40,000 on their mortgage and Zalman opted to work longer hours to make additional repayments to speed up their debt reduction. They currently have savings of $5,000, which will be used to pay for more house improvements.

Questions and answers: Nicole

What were the reasons you decided to go on the show?

We weren't getting anywhere financially. We were living on one income with a baby. We weren't struggling, but we weren't moving forward either.

How were you feeling about your financial position at the time?

I felt stuck in a rut.

How has your life changed since being on the show?

We have learnt to live by sticking to a budget and don't even notice it now; it's just become the norm for us. We are debt-free (other than our mortgage).

What did you find the most difficult about the tasks the show gave you?

I found the most difficult thing was getting Zal to stick to the budget and give me his EFTPOS card back!

What did you find the easiest?

The budget! I had always thought it was a difficult thing to do and work out, but it was so easy.

What were the most important things you learnt, and why?

To treat Zal's overtime as a bonus and use it to pay off debt instead of saving it. That it's better to pay credit card debt than to have savings — now I know that's because of the interest rates. It's simple when someone explains it, but it's nerve-racking to not have the security of having savings for emergencies.

How do you feel about your financial position now?

We are really happy with our financial position now. I am still a stay-at-home mum to our two children and we are surviving just fine.

SERIES 2, EPISODE 9: ANDREW

Age	45
Assets	
• Boat	$30,000
• Savings	$1,140
Total	**$31,140**
Debts	
• Personal loans	$3,940
• HP	$412
Total	**$4,352**
Savings before the show	$0
Savings after the show	$1,600
Debt before the show	$4,352
Debt after the show	$325
Home owner	No

Financial improvements

Andrew has paid off most of his debt. He plans to have $2,500 in his savings by Christmas 2007, and $8,000 to $10,000 by August 2008, which would be halfway to a deposit on his own home. Andrew has started his own business and is doing really well.

Questions and answers: Andrew

What were the reasons you decided to go on the show?

I had reached a point where my money issues needed to be confronted in such a way that it would force a change in my thinking and attitude towards money, i.e. 'Put your hand up on national TV' and at the same time learn new skills with budgeting and saving money.

How were you feeling about your financial position at the time?

Very lost with everything, because I did not have a direction or plan and I was not achieving my goals.

How has your life changed since the show?

Since the show many things have changed in my life. The biggest by far is that now I work for myself. I have started my own company — this I put down to the conversations I had with Brendon Johnson and Peter Brebner, just truly great guys to bounce ideas off. Money is important, and the way we think about it; I now deal with money issues up front, don' t let things drag on, and my blasé attitude towards it no longer exists.

What did you find the most difficult about the tasks the show gave you?

All the tasks that I was given challenged me, they were to the point and well thought out. Without a doubt the toughest task for me was seeing my children being honest about their dad and the money issues. The kids have forgotten it, but not me — it has become the greatest piece of motivation I got out of the show.

What did you find the easiest?

Filming — I enjoyed working with [host] Brendon Johnson.

What were the most important things you learnt, and why?

That when we change the way we think about something in life (money included) we change everything, and in a nutshell that's what I got out of the show. And that it takes 21 days to form a habit and 21 days to break a habit, and people are creatures of habit, some good and some destructive, actually very destructive.

How do you feel about your financial position now?

In a much more relaxed frame of mind regarding my money goals for the future; the kids understand this. And having the confidence now to know you can be effective with money in a positive way — I now have a plan.

SERIES 2, EPISODE 3: EMILY

Age	22
Assets	
• Car	$1,500
• Savings	$2,000
Total	**$3,500**
Debts	
• Student loans	$9,500
• Credit cards	$1,400
Total	**$10,900**
Savings before the show	$2,000
Savings after the show	$2,000
Debt before the show	$10,900
Debt after the show	$0
Home owner	No

Financial improvements

Emily has bought and sold two houses since the programme, and when settlement takes place she will be debt-free, which includes paying off her credit card and student loan.

Questions and answers: Emily

What were the reasons you decided to go on the show?

I had had enough of being broke and not being able to save for my future as well as doing the things I want to do right now.

How were you feeling about your financial position at the time?

I felt like I was going nowhere, and felt terrible every time I had to turn down an opportunity because of my lack of money. It can definitely get you down.

How has your life changed since being on the show?

I made lots of contacts and got involved in property investing, which was one of my goals. The show made me realise there's so much more to do, and money is a lot easier to come by, but also that you don't need money to enjoy yourself!

What did you find the most difficult about the tasks the show gave you?

Just generally sticking to the budget! It was all very new and seemed really hard at first, and then I saw my money accumulating and was very pleased with the results. I also had to give up a few luxury items which I found a bit difficult.

What did you find the easiest?

Having opportunities become more readily available! Experiencing the rewards of saving and working hard.

What were the most important things you learnt, and why?

I learnt how important budgeting is, mainly because I wasn't very good at it before and I spent all my money on things I could not account for.

Making sure I pay myself at least a small amount each payday before paying my bills.

Also that you need to go out and get things, because if you sit around they definitely won't come to you!

How do you feel about your financial position now?

I was doing really well for ages and then slipped back into my routine for a while. I'm now back on track and have definitely learnt my lesson, that old habits die hard and I need to kick them if I want to achieve my goals! I am definitely keen to stay on the right track as I've had a taste of what it can be like and am excited about improving my finances even more! I got a promotion and a pay rise. I've traded two houses, which helped pay off bills and go towards some really beneficial courses.

SERIES 2, EPISODE 5: MARJKA

Age	30
Assets	
• Home	$175,000
• Car	$12,000
Total	**$187,000**
Debts	
• Mortgage	$100,000
• Credit card	$122
• Car loan	$11,511
• Personal loan	$3,100
Total	**$114,733**
Savings before the show	$0
Savings after the show	$1,000
Debt before the show	$114,733
Debt after the show	$108,000
Home owner	Yes

Financial improvement

Marjka has learnt a lot from *Money Man*. She now looks at all her spending differently, and has made a list of the accounts she needs to reassess, such as her Vodafone plan, and her home phone line and Internet.

Her goal in the future is to set up her own business. She also owns half a house with an ex-boyfriend, and she hopes to buy him out so she owns the house freehold.

Questions and answers: Marjka

What were the reasons you decided to go on the show?

For financial advice and to force change in my out-of-control spending lifestyle.

How were you feeling about your financial position at the time?

I wasn' t feeling good about my financial position. I was stressed and worried.

How has your life changed since being on the show?

As soon as I get paid, I pay my bills straight away before spending any money on myself. I have looked at savings plans, investments and running my own business.

What did you find the most difficult about the tasks the show gave you?

Being on a strict budget, having to say no to social events if they were too expensive and living within my means.

What did you find the easiest?

Buying groceries every week instead of eating out was a good money-saver.

What were the most important things you learnt, and why?

If you want something you should save up for it; you pay so much more back in interest that it is just not worth it financially, let alone the stress you add to your life.

How do you feel about your financial position now?

I feel I am more in control of my finances, and I know I will never let myself get into debt again.

SERIES 2, EPISODE 5: PATRINA

Financial improvement

Patrina's entrepreneurial spirit has been unleashed since the show. She has built up her modelling business and is in the process of selling it. Her confidence in her abilities has increased dramatically. Patrina has tapped into her creative side and has come up with many great business ideas. By leveraging off her network, she has started developing those ideas. Her latest project, the *Wings and Wheels 2009 Calendar*, is due to be launched in March. These new business ventures have the potential to put her in a favourable financial position. With the basic money management strategies she learnt on the show and increased confidence in her capabilities, Patrina is well on her way to achieving financial freedom.

Patrina does not want the figures to be published.

Questions and answers: Patrina

What were the reasons you decided to go on the show?

To learn more about money and to get more TV experience.

How were you feeling about your financial position at the time?

Not good.

How has your life changed since being on the show?

I am on a money-making mission! My confidence has grown and I am taking control not only of my finances, but my life!

What did you find the most difficult about the tasks the show gave you?

Saving and going without. Actually having to watch what I spend.

What did you find the easiest?

I found the savings tips the easiest.

What were the most important things you learnt, and why?

In order to get ahead in life, you have to start today.

How do you feel about your financial position now?

I have started a new business, which I plan to grow and sell in a few years' time. I am on a money-making mission and feel confident that I will succeed!

GLOSSARY

Annuity

A retirement-income investment, where an individual invests their superannuation money and receives income periodically. The value of the account depends on the investment earnings and the amount of income taken. The capital is accessible and the income is flexible. There is no guarantee that the income will be paid for life.

Appreciation

The increase in the value of an asset.

Assets

A range of financial securities, such as shares, bonds, property, cash, savings and cars.

Balance sheet

A statement of assets, liabilities and nett equity, for an individual or any other entity, at a particular point in time.

Balloon payment

A large one-off loan repayment to clear a debt. Typical at the end of an interest-only term.

Baycorp

An association that lenders subscribe to which holds credit information on all of us. For a small fee, individuals can obtain a copy of their personal credit history from Baycorp. Under the

Privacy Act, it is also your right to have any erroneous data held on Baycorp files corrected.

Break costs
Penalties charged when a loan is paid off before the end of its term. Generally applies to fixed-rate loans.

Budget
An estimate, often itemised, of expected income and expenses for a given period in the future. Also a plan of operations based on such an estimate.

Capital gain
The monetary gain obtained when you sell an asset for more than you paid for it.

Cash
One of the asset classes. Coin and note currency in circulation, and in deposit accounts and money-market securities.

Compound interest
Interest that is paid on accumulated interest as well as on the original principal.

Conditional finance
See **Preapproved finance.**

Credit limit
The maximum amount of funds a borrower may have on an account, e.g. a credit card account.

Default

As a noun: an adverse entry on your credit report, showing that you have not paid a bill or invoice when due.

As a verb: the action of defaulting or not making a payment when due (e.g. failing to make loan repayments on time).

Disability or income-replacement insurance

Insurance that provides an income for the policyholder during a prolonged period of disability following sickness or an accident.

Disposable income

Any income left over after all known expenses have been met, e.g. mortgage payments, bills.

Diversification

Spreading an investment over a range of asset classes, sectors and regions with the aim of reducing risk. As the old saying goes, 'Don't put all your eggs in one basket.'

Draw down

To access available loan funds, especially lines of credit where the limit is set and you can use the funds as required.

Emergency fund

An amount set aside (usually the equivalent of three months' expenditure, sometimes six months') in highly liquid investments to meet unforeseen emergencies. The idea is to avoid having to liquidate other investments and risk financial loss.

Enduring Power of Attorney

A legal document that enables you to appoint a person or organisation to look after you and your affairs for the rest of your life regardless of the state of your physical or mental health.

Equity

The difference between the value of a property and what you owe to the bank or other lender(s); e.g. value $500,000; first mortgage $250,000, second mortgage $50,000. Equity is $200,000.

Fixed interest rate

An interest rate set for a fixed term. The rate cannot move (up or down) during the fixed term period. Penalties usually apply if the loan is repaid before the term expires. Fixed rates are generally available for terms of six months, or one, two, three, four and five years (although specials may apply for different periods).

Floating interest rate (or variable interest rate)

An interest rate that varies during the term of the loan. This rate can go both up and down, in line with movements in wholesale interest rates (usually the 90-day bank bill rate).

Fund manager

A person who invests money on behalf of unit holders (see **Unit trust**).

Gearing

The ratio of borrowed funds to the total value of a home or investment property (e.g., if you buy a property for $200,000, putting in a 20% deposit ($40,000), your gearing ratio is 80%).

Guarantee

A form of security for a loan where someone else promises/
guarantees to repay the loan if the borrower defaults. Lenders
view these as a poor form of security because of the bad
publicity that usually results for them if the guarantee has to be
exercised. These are typically required by a lender as a sign of
good faith by the borrower.

Guarantor

A party who agrees to be responsible for the payment of another
party's debts (see **Guarantee**).

Income statement

A statement of income and expenditure for a period, usually a
year (also called a profit and loss statement).

Inflation

The situation of excess money in circulation relative to the goods
and services available for purchase. Reflected in increasing prices.

Interest

The return earned on money that has been invested or loaned;
the price paid for its use.

Interest-only loan

A loan where the principal is repaid at the end of the loan term,
and interest only is repaid during the term of the loan. These loans
are usually short term, say one to five years. They are typically
favoured by property investors who wish to keep their loan
payments as low as possible. Compare **Principal and interest loan**.

Intestacy

The situation that occurs when a deceased person has made no will that disposes of all or some of their assets on death. The person is referred to as being 'intestate'.

Investment

An asset purchased with the intention of producing capital growth, or income, or both, for the owner.

Judgement

The next step after a **Default**, where the lender applies to the court and obtains a judgement to recover the outstanding debt.

Lease

A document granting a period of tenancy of a property under specific terms and conditions.

Lenders Mortgage Insurance (LMI)

When a deposit is under 20% of the purchase price, all lenders either insure the mortgage and charge an LMI premium, or alternatively take on the risk themselves and charge a 'low-equity fee'. Most banks insure the mortgage with an insurance company. The fees are calculated on a sliding scale: the lower your deposit, the higher the fee. Fees typically range between 0.5% and 1.5% of the loan amount. The premium is a one-off fee, and can usually be added to the loan amount.

Leverage

The use of borrowed capital to increase the potential return on an investment. Borrowing capital adds risk — if an investor uses leverage to fund an investment and the investment moves against them, the loss is much greater than it would have been if the investment were not leveraged — leverage magnifies not only gains, but also losses.

Liabilities

What a person owes (e.g., mortgages, credit card debts, personal loans, hire purchase, etc). There are also 'contingent liabilities', which are liabilities that are contingent on something happening, such as where a guarantee is acted upon through a loan default (in other words the liability may or may not come into effect).

Life insurance

The contractual obligation to make a payment in the event of certain contingencies — either the death of the person whose life is insured, or maturity of the policy.

Liquid assets

Assets in the form of cash, or that can be converted into cash at short notice.

Loan structure

The mixture of fixed-rate loans, floating-rate loans, and/or revolving-credit loans that make up the total amount borrowed. Loan structures are designed specifically for each client's individual circumstances.

Loan to valuation ratio (LVR)

The ratio of the amount lent to the value of the security offered or held. Commonly called the LVR. As a general rule, mortgage loans that exceed an LVR of 80% require lenders' mortgage insurance (see also **Gearing**).

Mortgage

A form of security for a loan usually taken over real estate. The lender (the mortgagee) has the right to take the real estate if the mortgagor fails to repay the loan.

Mortgage broker

A person or organisation that offers a service in which they select the best loan or loans for borrowers from a panel of lenders.

Mortgagee

See **Mortgage**; the lender of the funds.

Mortgagor

See **Mortgage**; the borrower of the funds.

Negative gearing

Where an investment is geared (usually to 100%) to produce a tax loss (e.g. where the total income from rent is less than the total outgoings, including mortgage payments, rates, insurance, etc., and depreciation). This loss may be able to be deducted from other taxable income.

Nett asset value

The value of a company or managed fund; i.e. the value of its assets less the value of its liabilities.

Nett worth

Calculated by subtracting total liabilities from total assets.

'No financials' loan

A loan where you do not have to provide proof of income (such as annual accounts, income statements, rental statements, etc.). It is only available to self-employed borrowers (including rental investors). Special conditions apply, but it is ideal when you have a new business, or when your annual accounts do not show an adequate capacity to service proposed debt. Loans MUST be secured by residential property only (not commercial).

Official cash rate (OCR)

The overnight base interest rate at which the Reserve Bank of New Zealand lends to, or borrows from, registered banks.

Portfolio

The full range of an investor's, or managed fund's, investment holdings.

Portfolio Investment Entity or PIE

A PIE is a new type of entity (such as a managed fund) that invests contributions in a range of different types of investment. PIEs came into existence on 1 October 2007. The entities will pay tax on investment income based on the prescribed investor rate (PIR) of their investors, rather than at the flat rate of 33%.

Preapproved finance

Finance that has been approved by a lender prior to the borrower finding a specific property to buy. Preapproved finance is typically conditional finance.

Principal

The borrowed amount of a debt or investment, on which interest is calculated.

Principal and interest loan (P&I)

A loan where both the principal and the interest are repaid together on a regular basis, by monthly or fortnightly instalments. Compare **Interest-only loan**.

Profit

Occurs when an investment appreciates in value and is sold, or realised. Also known as a realised gain.

Refinance

To replace or extend an existing loan with a new loan from the same or a different lender.

Return

The amount of money received from an investment each year. Can be made up of income and/or capital growth, and is usually expressed as a percentage of the investment.

Revolving-credit mortgage

A flexible loan arrangement with a specified ceiling, to be used at a customer's discretion.

Risk

The variability of returns. Generally, the higher the level of risk an investor is prepared to accept, the higher the potential return over time is likely to be.

Risk profile

A person's tolerance to risk.

Salary sacrifice

The amount of pre-tax salary an employee decides to contribute to a superannuation fund or allocate to a fringe benefit instead of taking it as cash salary.

Sale and purchase agreement

A written agreement outlining the terms and conditions for the purchase or sale of property.

Security

An asset that guarantees a loan to the lender until it is fully repaid. Usually property such as real estate is offered as security.

Term

The period of a loan, generally measured in years. A loan such as a mortgage can be for any period up to 30 years.

Trauma cover

A type of health insurance that covers the medical and other costs involved with certain medical conditions, operations, etc. It is paid as a lump sum.

Unit trust

An investment where a number of individuals place their money with a professional manager who manages the total fund on their behalf. Also known as a pooled investment or managed investment.

Whole-of-life insurance

Also called permanent insurance. The life insurance company pays out to the policyholder's beneficiary the sum for which they are insured (the basic sum assured), plus bonuses the policy has generated, when the policyholder dies.

Will

A statement as to how a person's property is to be distributed or disposed of on their death.

Yield

The dividend, or interest rate, on an investment expressed as a percentage of its price.

USEFUL WEBSITES

www.cab.org.nz Citizens Advice Bureau

www.consumer.org.nz An organisation that aims to get a fairer deal for consumers

www.familybudgeting.org.nz An organisation that offers free budgeting advice

www.goodreturns.co.nz Online money management magazine

www.ifa.org.nz Institute of Financial Advisors

www.ird.govt.nz/studentloans Inland Revenue site, with a guide to student loans

www.kiwisaver.govt.nz Guide to KiwiSaver

www.moneyTV.co.nz Financial education and tips in video format

www.retirement.org.nz Official government retirement site

www.simplesavings.co.nz Money-saving tips

www.sorted.org.nz Government financial education site

ABOUT THE AUTHOR

Lisa Dudson, ASM, CFP, BBS, GradDipBusStud (Personal Financial Planning) is a Certified Financial Planner. She is a director of Acumen Inc., a leading financial consulting company, and a director of the Avana Group, which provides high-quality investment properties for people looking to build long-term wealth. She is also the co-founder of the newly launched and rapidly growing website www.moneyTV.co.nz which offers free tips and information on personal finance and investing.

Lisa was the winner of the 2003 Young Financial Planner of the Year, and formerly vice-president of the Auckland Property Investors Association and the New Zealand Property Investors Federation, and secretary of the Auckland Institute of Financial Advisers. She appears regularly on TV, radio and in magazines, and is sought after as a speaker.

Lisa is a successful investor who offers practical advice based on her industry expertise and the strategies she has herself used. She is committed to delivering quality investment advice to enable her clients to achieve their lifetime financial goals.

www.acumen.co.nz
www.avanaproperties.co.nz
www.moneyTV.co.nz

Other books by Lisa Dudson

MoneyTV

Now you have read the book, see Lisa Dudson on TV on
www.moneyTV.co.nz

www.moneyTV.co.nz is a website that features short video
clips of Lisa and other experts offering financial management
tips just like the ones in this book.

www.moneyTV.co.nz is dedicated to giving you the financial
knowledge to move from where you are now to where you want
to be. As this book explains, for many this starts with getting their
spending patterns in order, while for others it's learning how to
manage debt, and for some it's deciding on a property-investment
strategy, a family trust or how to structure the best mortgage.

www.moneyTV.co.nz gives you insights into all these financial
issues, and a lot more, by offering access to New Zealand's
leading experts in each field. Delivered in concise three-to-
five-minute video clips, the site is searchable by topic or area
of concern.

Supporting the video clips are in-depth articles and an
online bookstore for financial and investment-related books.
There is also a section called 'Ask an Expert', where viewers are
able to suggest topics that Lisa can respond to by video.

Registering your name on the site means that every week
you will be emailed a link to the latest free video clips posted
on the site.

ABOUT THE CREATORS OF MONEY MAN

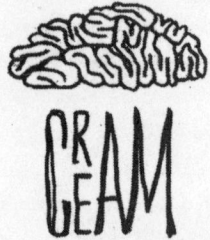

Cream Media is a New Zealand-based hothouse for the best in factual entertainment, comedy and formats that the break the mould. The creative folk at Cream also produce corporate videos, DVD and interactive media.

The Cream team is responsible for some of the best — and highest-rating — shows in the country. They have reached in to the heart and soul of New Zealand and beyond, with shows including *Auction House, Borderline, Border Patrol, Coast Watch* and, of course, *Money Man*.

For more information about Cream Media, or if you would like to order the Money Man series go to **www.creammedia.co.nz.**

INDEX